MW01243175

Riding The Bus 1

Luis Pástor Villalobos

Printed in the United States of America.

ISBN-10: 1490928545
ISBN-13: 978-1490928548
Order books on www.createspace.com/4351776

DEDICATION

I can't continue without saying thank you. First, I would like to thank my Lord Jesus Christ who gave me the vision to transfer my thoughts to my LUCKY PEN, then to the paper and finally to the publication of my first book. Thank you to the fallen economy which taught me (I chose to learn) that money needs to be spent wisely, to stay away from credit. Thank you to the public transportation system which serves as an avenue to save money and to conserve clean air. I have to thank the people on the bus who gave me the inspiration to write about the monotony and the beauty of riding the bus all at the same time. Thank you to education and to my students who have taught me to dream and expect the best. Thank you to ITC International which has given me the opportunity to take my students and my son on unforgettable educational journeys throughout the world. Thank you to John Cummuta and his Debt into Wealth Program and Bill Cherry, my coach, who catapulted me into debt freedom and my first published book. I must show my gratitude to countless friends and colleagues who have given me ample ideas and encouragement to continue with my project. Special thanks to Mr. Marin who has offered to provide black and white pictures for my future poems. Very special thanks to my daughter Tanya who touched up my picture on my back cover. Thank you to the rest of my immediate and extended family which gave me the inspiration to write about their struggles and triumphs. Finally, but not lastly, (and this happened just two days ago) I would like to thank my dear wife who showed faith in by book by asking me to hurry up and publish my book. She too has dreams wants to pursue and accomplish them.

TABLE OF CONTENTS

PREFACE

One of the rules I made for writing this book was that I would write my poems only on the bus, thus the name of the book, "Riding the Bus". I was sitting at Burger King waiting for my son to return from symphony practice and I decided I would write the prelude to my first book. I began by writing, "I am like most people". Then I got writer's block. What could such a statement mean? I am like most people, but I am also NOT like most people. I have just as many things in common as uncommon with others. I am unique in my own right, probably just like anyone else.

I like this introduction a lot better (I am riding the bus and writing on the bus) than a blank statement, "I am like most people". If this book is going to serve its purpose it is going to explore the phenomenon of life: diversity, hope, faith, past, present, and the future. It is my hope that the reader will be challenged to think about his/her own life, pick up a LUCKY PEN and make history on paper.

I'd like to fill a few lines to tell you about the birth of my book. Two things: the economy and people telling me I should write a book about my life. At LAUSD there have been several cutbacks, the last being an unprecedented 12 furlough days. When I returned from Paris, France with my students I realized that not once had I driven a car while there. My students and I were doing only what rich people do, all by public transportation: airplanes, trains, buses, taxis and on foot. Faced with the need for new tires, car repair and more money, it was then that I decided that I would ride the bus to save money to buy tires. The ball kept rolling and eventually I sold my car and I have begun using the money I am saving to pay off all my debts, beginning with my smallest. Please pay close attention to two of my poems that will reflect the duel birth of my book: "You shouldn't be a teacher" and "Bad things happen".

The central themes of my book are God, family, education and the economy. At times it is difficult to separate the four since they are very much related and intertwined. God is present in the other three in that I have to trust God for the progress of my family, as a teacher I feel committed, and money is necessary to get ahead in life.

Although I cannot say my book is a Christian book or for a Christian audience, I make no excuses for my being a Christian. Nevertheless, faith is a central theme in any religion or in any dreams, goals that we may have in life. In my opinion, even atheists believe in something. Atheism is a philosophy and it must be embraced if someone chooses to live by it. Even atheism teaches respect for other people's beliefs.

As a teacher I feel a calling to inspire students. When I was a child, a teenager, and even in college it was often my teachers who encouraged me to go on. Many of my poems have to do with my experience as a student and my experiences as a teacher. In one of my poems I mention that many students see school as a home away from home. It is a great responsibility for anyone who enters the career of education. Education requires both hard work and dedication not only from the student but from the teacher as well.

The family is the first school that anyone attends. If the home structure is inadequate it is extremely difficult for individuals to come out ahead. It is in the home where a child needs to learn values such as respect for all races, respect for adults, the value of hard work and ethics, how to handle money. Unfortunately, it is in the home where people learn the wrong lessons. Many parents were not taught correctly, consequently they teach their children to hate, cheat, steal, and squander money. I am from a dysfunctional family and many of my poems will attest to that. It is no surprise that I am the only college graduate out of seven children.

Lastly, the economy is instrumental to success in any of the other three themes. Sometimes it is difficult for a person who has little money or someone who has a lot of money to believe in God. Money is a good tool to be used to help a family come out ahead. Such a tool need not be measured in millions but in quality. The proper management of money is learned. I have made it my goal at age 54 to learn how money can work for me.

This book is about dreams and dreams coming true. So, I will venture to say and dream that those who read my poems will somehow be inspired to make positive changes in their lives. I encourage the reader to leave the past behind and move forward. Set high goals and make it your intention to accomplish them. Now, read my poems, be inspired and inspire others.

HIGHLIGHTS

Every time I pick up my book and want to share my favorite poems it is difficult to choose one because I think they are all pretty good. Each one carries a message, reflection or moral issue. Nevertheless, there are some poems that seem to stand out to more than one reader. Every poem and every reader become connected in their own special way. Please allow me to share a few of those poems that seem to send a special message of hope and inspiration.

First of all, let's just talk about simply the practice of riding the bus, although other themes may be involved. Certain poems such as "100 years", "Bus Stop" and "Smells" capitalize on the act of riding the bus, but at the same time they are inspirational and they do have a bit of the other themes as well. For example, "100 years" emphasizes the importance of physical exercise and how riding the bus affords me the opportunity to get my well-deserved and necessary exercise. "Smells" on the other hand talks about the discomfort that a rider may experience, while at the same time saving money on gasoline and car repair. On the philosophical and spiritual side, "Bus Stop" opens the door to thought and reflection. It is during those quiet moments, when people can take the time to think and make important life decisions.

To expound on the concept of the economy let's look at a few poems that may pertain to the financial aspect of my poetry: "Chase bank", "Credit card" and "My choice". "Chase bank" is one of those epic poems that move a person to make hard decisions. I knew that my economic situation was not going to improve unless I did something drastic. The use of credit is out of control in our society and "Credit card" emphasizes the importance of paying cash and buy only those things you can afford, without using credit. Finally, I believe that life is a series of choices. An individual can choose to ride the bus, or be forced and unhappy with using public transportation.

Education may be one of the most important factors that influence our economic status. "A wiener" is a story of a student who came to the USA to succeed. People with college degrees usually land better jobs and lead an improved life style. I am committed to education and "I am a teacher" proves that I have a passion for affecting teens in a positive way. Too many teens fail to realize that education and a professional career can make the difference in the future. "Suffer or suffer" is dedicated to those students who take education seriously and to those students who need to get on the right track.

Our families are affected by our educational level and, consequently, our economic standing. My mother was one of those people who gave me the drive to become educated. She encouraged me every chance she got to go for the impossible. Sometimes I joke that, if I had chosen to be a thief, my mother would have told me to be one of the best. "An angel" shows how my mother was instrumental in my success as a student. As a father I have a great responsibility to help my own children come out ahead. "I am a father" is about being committed to our children. I can't finish this paragraph, though, without saying that I love my wife. "I love my wife" is a token of the love I feel for my wife.

Finally, faith in God, in my opinion is the single most important element of success in life. Even if you don't want to believe, you still have faith. "Faith" is a poem that demonstrates that everyone has faith in something. Without being blunt, but I want to be honest; I am a Christian. "In the name of Jesus" uncovers the drive that I have in my life to get things done. "Man up!" explores what can happen when people want to take control without regard for God or others. We live on this earth to share our lives with others not to fly solo.

100 YEARS (1)

Rational: Months after riding the bus to work I realized that I was getting the type of workout that health spa members only dream of. I walk several minutes in the morning to reach my bus stop and repeat the process in the afternoon. As my poem attests I often have to run to catch the bus. There have been times when I caught the bus just in time, and other times I have seen the bus ride away. Some bus drivers have the heart to wait a few seconds and other drivers just drive away.

100 YEARS (1)

Several times I have had to run
A short distance to catch the bus.
I am 54 but I run like 20.

From a distance I can see or hear
The bus approaching its stop
Or I'm late and I have to run to catch the bus.

Like a young kid, running like crazy
I put myself in first and second gear
Lugging my bags along.

Gasping for air I board the bus
And in several occasions
I have told the bus driver,

"If I live to be 100, I will owe it all to public transportation."
The drivers who don't stop or might not see me running,
Will never receive the pleasure of hearing these words
And seeing an old man gasp for air.

21 WAYS TO SAY I LOVE YOU (2)

Message: Love is such a complicated subject. Too many of us don't say I love you enough while few of us say it too much. I believe you should always say I love you in as many ways you can. When I was dating my wife I made her, her very own "I love you" card which she still has to this day. If you love someone don't live your life regretting you never said I love you.

21 WAYS TO SAY I LOVE YOU (2)

"Ana bahibik", the elderly Arabic man shouted,
As I walked up to pay for my gasoline.
"Ana bahibik", I followed.
No one really knew what we were saying.

"Mayatoom say piar carta hoon", Punjabi,
My favorite way to say I love you.
I thank my Indian students
For teaching me such beautiful words.

Throughout the first couple of months
That I learned to love my then girlfriend, my future wife,
I made it customary to ask everyone
How to say I love in their mother tongue.

Finally, 21 ways to say I love you,
A love letter that I sent
To my then precious girlfriend.
18 years later, I still say, "te quiero".

To date I have continued the tradition.
I am up to about 40 ways now.
Thank you to my Jewish friend, Moti
Who encouraged me to say, "anee ohev otah".

65 YEAR OLD "CHOLO" (3)

Moral: This is a funny but sad story of a man who lives out his life as an old gang banger. In the Hispanic community we refer to these men as "veteranos", men who have a history of gang affiliation. I thought the elderly man featured on this poem should have a gun in his pocket because he didn't stand a chance in a fist fight. Months later I saw the same man drunk as a whistle and he fell on the sidewalk as he got off the bus. Those who are wise and read this poem will make a 180 degrees turn in fear of ending life as a washed out veterano, riding the bus not by personal choice but by necessity.

65 YEAR OLD "CHOLO" (3)

Khaki pants
Spit-shined patent leather shoes.
Plaid shirt, hanging out
And buttoned all the way to the top.
"Blankin Little Larry is doing
Blankin time in the blankin pen again!"
He screamed to someone at the back of the bus.

Four letter words
Coming out of his mouth
Every two or three words.

He is standing at the front of the bus
Obstructing traffic
Although there are empty seats.

"Don't step on my shoes, vato!",
As an obese man walks by.
At what age does a man stop
Trying to be hard like a cholo?

A WIENER (4)

Reflection: This is one of my favorite poems, but of course I say this about all of them. This one tells the story of one of my former students who had a goal and didn't give up until she accomplished it. I told her that she had to be friends with students who did not speak Spanish. If she associated with students like herself she would be speaking Spanish only and would not advance in her English skills. To my surprise she did just what I asked her to do. With the help of all her teachers and her determination to succeed she became the number one student and was accepted to her dream school, UCLA. Weeks before graduation I saw her walk with her English-speaking friend and off to the movies.

A WIENER (4)

"This is what wieners are made of"
The valedictorian said proudly.
She could not pronounce the word, winners.

I remember when she first came to my high school.
"I came to this country in the trunk of a car.
God brought me to this country for a reason."
From that moment she decided
That she would become valedictorian.
She learned to speak English like a bullet.

She quickly moved from my ESL class
To ESL 2 and 3, kept pressing on,
Until she finished regular English by the end of 9th grade.

She was 17 by the time she enrolled, by age 20
She was at the podium presenting her eloquent speech.
"Wieners are made of scrap meat
And winners are made of hard work and dedication."

ABUSED (5)

Moral: This poem is dedicated to those people who are suffering from the effects of a life that was not their choice. They became victims of their environment, their offenders. What matters is what will happen to these people for the rest of their lives. It took a cartoon for me, The Lion King, to realize that the past is not important when an individual wants to move forward. I tell my students that although life may be difficult it is not an excuse to stop trying.

ABUSED (5)

Abused, accused, neglected, molested?
So, go on with your life, it's in the past.
It hurts? Get counseling, pray, get help.

The drugs, the alcohol, the sex?
Let go, they're not your friends.
Let go of the past, your anger, regret and sorrow.

Hate the offender? Ok, forgive.
It's not your fault, you're not to blame.
Don't get help, forgive, and forget? That's your mistake.

Divorced parents? You, get a good marriage.
Lost a loved one? Go get another one.
No money? Get education. Learn how money works.

Listen, everyone makes mistakes.
Learn from your mistakes.
"You have to put the past behind you",

A great philosopher once said,
As the camera selectively zeroed in on his butt,
His name was Pumbaa.

AN ANGEL (6)

Reflection: We all have parents who are unique. They represent a part of us that sets us apart from everyone. Most of us hold our parents very dear, provided they were not abusive or neglected us when we were children. Unlike my father, my mother was always there through thick and thin. Although she was not perfect by any means, she had a heart of gold. My mother taught me that our world can be whatever we make it to be.

AN ANGEL (6)

If you slapped her, she would think
That you were caressing her.
If you insulted her she thought
You were giving her a complement.

She didn't see the evil in people
Because she wasn't looking for it.
She was innocent, and full of heart.
She believed anything and everything.

People might criticize my mother
For not teaching me the dangers of life
But she lived in her own world, her reality.
Doesn't everyone choose to believe?
I thank God for my mother.
She taught me to believe in the impossible.
To be able to walk on clouds.
Now, she is walking on clouds, since 4/4/4

I was born of an angel.

ANGELIC MOTHER (7)

Reflection: The name of this poem comes from the City of Angeles, Los Angeles. I came to Los Angeles, a total stranger, looking for a place to settle down. I was received into this family as a renter with open arms, later became a member of the family church and soon like a member of the family. Our Christian faith kept us all closely knit to the point that I came to see both she and her husband as my parents. To this day I stay in contact and my children see them as grandparents.

ANGELIC MOTHER (7)

Mothers, I've had two.
My maternal mother and one in LA.
She would cook for me
And wash for me like a son.

She would give me advice, encouragement.
She helped me with my faith in God
Chilaquiles with chorizo, um, um
Tortillas, beans, rise and cheese, um, um

I was like a member of the family.
Family parties, I was there.
She presented me to friends
As another one of her sons.

I thank God for my angelic mother.
Not too many men can boast of having two.
One day both mothers met,
And they were like friends.

BAD THINGS HAPPEN (8)

Message: This is one of the very first poems I wrote when I started riding the bus in April of 2010. I was optimistic about my decision to ride the bus to save money and start paying off my debt. LAUSD was going into its third year of major cutbacks in education. It took me two years to realize that I couldn't continue living as in the past. The fallen economy made me realize that I was using credit irresponsibly to buy things that I couldn't afford and really didn't need. If you look at life from a positive point of view there is always a lesson to learn from any shortcoming that may ensue.

BAD THINGS HAPPEN (8)

Bad things happen for good reasons.
It all depends how you see, deal with them.
No summer school, 12 furlough days
No after school programs, no money.

The economy is bad, but I'm good!
I'm riding the bus, 84 dollars a month.
I'm rich! God is holding my money.
He's giving it to me slowly, more than I can imagine.

There will be better days, I believe,
The birds eat, the flowers get dressed.
God loves animals and trees.
How much more does he love me?

I am writing this book and giving it to God.
He is going to pay me back over a long period of time.

Residual income.

BEGGAR (9)

Message: Since I wrote this poem about two years ago, my oldest brother has since gotten his own place to live. He was found on the street agonizing from abdominal pain and was taken to the emergency room near death. My other brother is still in the streets of Tijuana drinking himself to sleep and letting his head drop where it may. He is hooked on substance addiction and there seems to be no end. Nevertheless, I still pray and hope that one day a miracle will happen to him as well.

BEGGAR (9)

"Do you have some spare change, sir?"
The beggar asks me at the bus stop.
I always give a dollar or spare change.
I think of my two homeless brothers.

I don't know what the beggar will do,
Smoke it, shoot it, not my concern.
I have a duty on to God
To help the poor and destitute.

Always be thankful for what you have.
Never pass judgment on a beggar.
You don't know what turns his life took.
The way the economy is now, anybody can lose anything.

Next time you meet a beggar
Give him/her some spare change.
You can't be sure he is in a scam.
She may be truly hungry and homeless.

BELIEVE ME (10)

Reflection: This poem has to do with having faith in people. It is difficult to believe once you have been deceived, but faith should never end. Giving an individual a first chance and a second chance may make the difference between success and failure. We humans have the tendency to judge everyone and judge every event by one standard. Some people actually tell the truth some of the time. Sometimes it is good to trust in yourself, and others too.

BELIEVE ME (10)

Some people don't believe anything
While others believe everything
"I forgot my pass," I informed the bus driver.
"Bus regulations say you must show a pass or pay!"

Got off one bus, onto another.
"I forgot my pass at home," I said.
"I know you, I remember you from yesterday," he assured.
He let me by, trusted me and believed me.

Believe me. I was telling the truth
The first driver knew me too.
The same driver that screamed at me.
Some people believe you and others don't.

The second driver used his better judgment,
He had compassion and showed it.
What kind of person are you?
Do you give others a chance?

Have you ever, or will you ever?

BUS STOP (11)

Reflection: In today's daily life it seems like we do a lot but don't accomplish much. While waiting at the bus stop I get to experience my world in slow motion. I have time to think, to practice patience. I see people coming and going, cars passing by, more than 90 percent with only the driver. I often wonder about all these people, where they are going, what they are doing. Riding the bus has given me the time to just stop and think.

BUS STOP (11)

The bus is not the only thing that stops,
My life stops too.
And I have time to think.

I think about my wife, son, daughter, students.
I think about my challenges and triumphs.
I have time to listen to the birds,

Compose their morning songs,
To think about what I am thinking.
Stop. Slow down.

Now you have time,
To listen to the birds sing,
To watch the world pass by.

I think that man is going to work too.
I think that woman has problems too.

Stop and pray, stop and think,
You now have time to stop.

CAN'T WAIT!!! (12)

Message: Sometimes it is hard to wait for something you truly want. For example, you may be anticipating the final outcome of a long-awaited project; waiting for a loved one. Are there things you want to do in life? Have you started them and are excited to reach the end. This type of impatience might not be so bad; the desire to win in life.

CAN'T WAIT!!! (12)

Can't wait! I can see the end.
Excitement growing, hope rising.
The hard work is paying off.
Closing the finish line.

Enthusiasm, exhilarating feelings.
I see the end so close.
I see progress being made.
My efforts are paying off.

I'm going to accomplish my goal.
I know I will, with God's help.
When I make my mind up
There is no stopping me.

I can't wait! to be debt free.
Can't wait! to go back to Europe
I can't wait! to have fluent speaking students
To have 100% pass the AP French test.

Can't wait to see my dream,
Come to an inevitable fruition.
Can't wait! to go celebrate.
To have dinner with the French President.

CAN'T WALK? CRAWL (13)

Reflection: There are times in life when things become so complicated that it is almost impossible to continue. During these times we have to stop, take a break and then continue the best way we can, never giving up. Babies crawl because they can't walk but they keep trying and trying until they start to walk, and what joy these bring to adults! I think what is important in life is not that you can't seem to keep going but that the pressures of life never made you give up.

CAN'T WALK? CRAWL (13)

There are moments in life
You can never forget.
Moments you should never forget.

I took the bowling ball, swung back,
With all my strength, moved forward
Let the ball go and fell flat on my back.

At the time I was attending a Christian college,
Hardcore, fundamentalist, totally intolerant.
I thought I had made a mistake and should leave.

Laughter broke out as people usually do
When someone takes a hard fall.
I hit the back of my head so hard that I couldn't move.

Then I heard this little voice.
"When you can't walk, crawl"
I turned over on my stomach and

Dragged myself across the floor.
Shortly thereafter I packed my bags
Flew back to LA, and crawled back to my old job.

CHASE BANK (14)

Rational: The birth of this poem was totally accidental just as all of my poems. I didn't plan any of them just as I didn't plan to doze off and wake up to a sign that read CHASE BANK. At that moment I felt God was speaking to me. I had no intention of staying on the bus for any long period of time and certainly not selling my car, but it was fate, God's will.

CHASE BANK (14)

Appropriate name for a bank
that is chasing me for my money
200 dollars a month, their Chrysler
if I stop paying, they take it away.

Until I finish paying, the car is not mine
they keep the pink slip for keepsake
they don't care that I am paying
almost twice as much as the original price.

The bonus checks the CEO's got
we paid them with our interest payments
I don't want to be chased anymore
I am paying off my Chrysler, no more credit.

I'm selling my Tacoma, I truly own it
take the money to pay off the Chrysler
save money every month to buy a new car
or just stay on my limo, M-Metro.

CRAVING A THANK YOU (15)

Moral: Have you ever done anything for someone and really didn't expect any recognition? I guess that's ok, but sometimes we get just the opposite. We humans generally take time to say what is wrong but rarely take notice of the good things. It seems that our society is becoming less concerned with showing gratitude. After a series of complaints, it's good to encounter someone who has something good to say. In that light I want to say thanks.

CRAVING A THANK YOU (15)

I said I was doing this for You and I was.
It was ok if no one acknowledged me.
But now I am craving a thank you.

A student who would say thank you.
Thank you for being my teacher.
Thank you for taking me to Europe.

A parent who would call to see how I am.
A teacher who would stop by to say thanks.
A wife, son, daughter, thank you.

People don't seem to say please and thank you.
Adults, need to practice the Barney principle.
Adults and teens need to show more gratitude.

Well, I'm going to take a moment to say thank you.
Thank you for buying and reading my book.
Thank you for making my dream come true.

Hope this book will bless you and others.
I hope someone will write to say thank you.
Thank you, Jesus, for helping me to publish this book.

CREDIT CARD (16)

Message: The use of credit is out of control in the U.S. We have become accustomed to fast-food, getting information quickly and instant gratification. In the long run this mentality is going to seriously hinder our own personal financial status and the economy of our world. My father used to tell me that I shouldn't buy anything if I didn't have the money on hand. I thought my father was old fashioned and didn't understand the nature of credit. My father was an intelligent man.

CREDIT CARD (16)

Buy now, pay later.
How much later?
How much more?

I need credit,
For the things I have accomplished,
For the things I have done.

I don't need credit
To charge things I can't afford.
I want credit for spending money wisely.

A credit card that says,
"Accomplished teacher and educator,
Accomplished father and husband".

I am going to pay off
All those credit cards that say
I owe money to other people.

I want a credit card
That says, "Job well done!"
I think I'm going to make me one.

DEEP SLEEPER (17)

Rational: One of the things I truly enjoy about riding the bus besides writing while riding is that I can fall asleep anytime. I couldn't do that while I was driving. In fact, twice I did fall asleep and was involved in two solo accidents, thank God, I didn't hurt anyone. This poem would be quite comical if you could see the video. This young man apparently did not sleep at home to be this sleepy, enough to bump his head and still keep sleeping. Nevertheless, we should not judge as I pointed out: anybody can fall asleep and bump their head on the railing of the bus.

DEEP SLEEPER (17)

Head and upper body
Completely swaying
To the right and left

Head comes down
Very close to his waist level
Nearly falls off the seat.

Sometimes he would lean forward
In the shape of a C
Bus brakes, hits his head hard on the railing.

I offered him my seat
Next to the window.
More room for his big feet.

Funny it seems, should not judge.
Weeks later, it happened to me
I was sleeping, bumped my head

Hard on the railing, more than once.

DON'T TAKE DRUGS (18)

Reflection: Can you think back to a time when you were bullied, or perhaps you were the bully? Look back and remember what it was like. How did you survive? Did you ever stoop down to the bully's level? I hope you are not being bullied now, but if you are, remember how you survived. Just like then the bully will grow up or time will pass.

DON'T TAKE DRUGS (18)

Throughout my school years
There was a bully who wanted to fight me.
He was big, obese, like a football player.

I always ignored him
He wasn't worth the trouble.
He got his kicks by bullying others.

Time went by, we both matured.
One day I walked past his house.
He shouted, "Hey Louie, don't do drugs!"

"Yea, alright man.
Take it easy!" I replied.
He was strung out on drugs.

You know, in life
You have to stand your ground
Until the bully grows up.

DREAMS COME TRUE (19)

Moral: If you never give up on yourself, others and your dream, eventually you'll have a major breakthrough. If you really want something you really have to work hard to get it. I never gave up on organizing trips to Europe for teens and now I am just months away from establishing my own 501 (c) 3 that will have its mission to provide educational travel for teens. This book you are now reading has been in the makings for over two years and I am not giving up.

DREAMS COME TRUE (19)

22 years of teaching,
I always wanted to take students to Europe,
As my own experience when I was 18.

Carwashes, bake sales, candy sales, dinners,
Sleepless nights, worries, problems, accusations,
Deception, wanting to give up, to forget the dream.

But I kept on, I had a duty to God.
I had a duty to the dream, to my students.
I kept on, didn't waver, went for the goal.

It happened. We went to Paris and Madrid.
Palacio Royal, Plaza Mayor, Parque del Retiro,
Tour Eiffel, Versailles, Champs-Élysées.

"Are you going to do this again?", I was asked.
"Well, if I was smart I would remember all the problems.
But I'm not smart so I'm doing it again" I replied.

Now we are fundraising for the French Promenade.
New group of students, new expectations.
This trip will be better than the first.

DRIVER 44744 (20)

Message: My experience as a bus rider began on a bad note. Bus drivers, like teachers and other professions that involve people services can become quite stressed when working with their clients. Sometimes we might overstep our authority which only increases stress for all. Since I am conscious of my own flaws I decided to remain calm as this bus driver tried to pick a fight with me. In the progressing months I witnessed unnecessary discussions between drivers and passengers. In this incident I chose to be chill and cool.

DRIVER 44744 (20)

I got off the ramp,
Walked across to bus 76,
Was given the finger to go back

Power! Behind his voice!
"You are not supposed to get off the ramp!
I could have run you over!"
The bus was stopped.

His job must be really hard,
To become so angry,
At a man much older than him.

I looked at his badge,
I looked at his raging face,
His fast-moving lips,

Should I report his disrespect to his boss?
Nah, forgive and forget,
I've made mistakes too,

My first day on the bus.

FACES (21)

Moral: In a world of so many people, so many walks of life, an individual has to find his place in this world. Faces tell stories of lives, experiences and dreams. While riding the bus I have had the opportunity to observe people and talk to all kinds of people. I have shared my poems with many on the bus and I have discovered that much like the freeway, the supermarket, your local church, you will find all kinds of people. I have met people who were in prison, recovered addicts and even professionals like me. Everyone has a story to tell.

FACES (21)

Same faces, familiar faces
Some sad, some serious and sleepy.
Cold stares, rarely smile.
I've talked to 2 or 3 so far.

I wonder about those faces:
Their stories, their experiences,
Everyone has a story to tell.

Some single, some divorced.
Single parents, I'm sure.
Students, retired people, disabled,
Some are reading, I am writing.

I wonder about their future.
Where are they going?
What are they doing?

Are they going to school, work, or visit?
I know where I am going,
And I know who I am.
I am rich, a son of a King!

FAITH (22)

Message: Wow! This is a deep and profound subject. Without faith you cannot believe in God or in anyone or anything else, for that matter. Without realizing it we exercise faith every day. When we get up, ride the bus or drive our car to work we exercise faith. In my community the freeway is under reconstruction and I see workers with power machines literally putting mountains where they didn't exist to build bridges across the freeway. I believe they are exercising their faith.

FAITH (22)

Faith can move mountains, the Bible says.
The biggest mountain is oneself.
When you know what to do, and you don't
Pray to move the biggest mountain ever.

The distance between A and B
Is the space in between.
You have to travel the road between.
Faith can turn obstacles into opportunities.

Faith can move mountains.
You are a mountain.
Your goals and dreams are mountains.
Believing is the beginning of reality.

Faith has already moved mountains.
Your birth, survival, growth, progress.
Grammar school, high school, college,
Marriage, children, prosperity

These are all mountains too.

GO BACK WHERE YOU... (23)

Reflection: Racism is an ugly human ailment. People seem to forget their roots, become territorial and will not let anyone in their space. The U.S. in particular is a country that is made up of foreigners from all over the world. Unfortunately, generation after generation, people forget that they are descendants of immigrants too. Native Americans and Native Mexicans, for example, are often considered outsiders.

GO BACK WHERE YOU... (23)

"You stupid Mexicans should
go back where you came from!"
the big White football player challenged.

I was always one
To fight with my brain.
Physical was reserved for the karate ring.

I looked up at him and replied.
"Ok, I'll go back where I came from
But you go back where you came from."

"I'll swim the Rio Grande
And you swim the Atlantic Ocean.
Let's see who gets home first."

This standoff happened
Almost 40 years ago.
It is sad that some people
Still think this way.

It is sad that the very descendants
Of this land are considered illegal.
Are we illegal aliens, extra-terrestrials?

GREAT, GREAT, GREAT, GREAT! (24)

Moral: This poem I consider the most insignificant because I didn't put much effort in its making. Nonetheless a couple of people have told me that this poem is one of their favorites. I guess everyone has a different interpretation of a text especially if they can identify with it. The message is pretty clear that people should put others first to reach inner peace. This particular day I was feeling pretty up in spirit and it was evident that I was not concerned about myself. I have found that when I dwell on myself and my problems I can fall into depression. On the other hand, if I spend time helping others I discover how fortunate I really am.

GREAT, GREAT, GREAT, GREAT (24)

"How are you doing today, Mr.?"
I'm doing great, great, great, great!
Then I began to think:
Never been better, I have a plan.

I'm doing great, I'm putting God first.
And He will bless me according to his abundance.
He will feed me, clothe me, as He sees fit.

I'm doing Great! I'm putting others second.
No time to feel sorry for myself.
There are people truly in need, who can use help.

I'm doing great? And I am last.
I have nothing to worry about.
My Lord is taking care of all my needs.

HOMELESS BROTHERS (25)

Message: This is a bit more information about my brothers: one a Vietnam veteran and the other a victim of drug abuse. How many of you have family members or know someone who is a war veteran? For some evident reason many of our soldiers develop long term social development problems. Many of our homeless are former members of our armed forces. My other brother is a different story: abuse, neglect, alcohol, and drug addiction. Please, be compassionate and care for the homeless.

HOMELESS BROTHERS (25)

I have two homeless brothers.
One is a Vietnam Veteran.
One deported to the streets of Mexico.

Life is not fair.
Why am I riding this bus?
Why is he eating out of garbage cans?

Life is not fair.
Why is he divorced, abandoned?
Why do I have a beautiful wife?

I have two brothers
Two homeless brothers
Two of millions of other homeless

I have a beautiful house
Air conditioning and heating,
Warm sheets and a comfortable bed.

I have two homeless brothers.
Are they hungry and thirsty today?
Will someone give them a warm bed tonight?

HOPE AT 40 (26)

Reflection: Some people believe that the number 3 is a lucky number, hence the saying, "third time is the charm". In life we may have to try something several times until we get it right. Perhaps a business deal went bad more than once, but you never gave up. This is the second time that I attempt to publish my book and I have a feeling this is the one for me too. Unfortunately, relationships go bad too often, as is the case of many marriages. I love and respect my niece very much and I am confident that this is the one too.

HOPE AT 40 (26)

She was 17 when she married,
Had 2 children with a man
Much older that her.

She wanted to leave home.
Marriage was the only way out.
But things didn't work out.

About 4 years later
She tried it again.
And had her third child.

Now she just turned 40.
She got married in a church
For the first time in her life.

The third time is a charm
"This is the one", she said.
I love my niece. I pray this one is it.

HURRY UP, MAN! (27)

Moral: Riding the bus has introduced me to a wide array of people and personalities. I have met professionals, day laborers and those who are downright undesirable. As in the case of this poem we compare and contrast two extremes of good and bad. Some people are struggling to weather out the fallen economy and others are just bitter and doomed to ride the bus. Life is whatever we perceive life to be.

HURRY UP, MAN! (27)

Remember I told you there are all kinds of people?
There are two extremes, north and south poles.
Some will kill you and some will save you.

There are those who complain, those who help.
Those who put you down, those who pick you up.
Some practice philanthropy, others theft.

A man on a wheelchair boarded the bus.
Could not adjust or secure his chair.
Thugs in the back complained, "Hurry up, man!"

The bus was delayed only five minutes.
What appointment were these thugs pressed to keep?
Insulting the bus driver and the disabled man.

After several unsuccessful attempts,
The man on the wheelchair had to get off.
"Only in LA, stupid bus drivers like you", the thugs exclaimed.

I AM A BROTHER (28)

Reflection: We are born into our family, perhaps not the ideal family we imagined. Our families are not perfect as we are not perfect. It took me some time to accept my family, to lose the shame of a fallen family. Now I have learned to accept my brothers and sisters for what they are without shame or remorse. I have learned to not feel superior because I am a college graduate.

I AM A BROTHER (28)

I am a brother of three brothers.
Brother of three sisters.
Only I graduated from college.

I am a brother with two homeless brothers.
I am a brother of two struggling sisters.
I am a proud brother of one of my sisters.

My mother and father came to this country
With their hopes and dreams in their hands.
They wanted a better future for their children.

I am the pride of my brothers.
The pride of my mother and father.
I am the pride of my extended family.

I am a brother, proud of my sister.
She is a private tutor, a very good one.
She was like a mother to me in my youth.

I am a brother, proud of my brother
He conquered serious drug addiction.
I am a brother, I thank God for my family.

I AM A CHRISTIAN (29)

Reflection: The next few poems explore my identity: what I am, what I stand for. I have accepted my role as a brother realizing that I can choose my friends but I cannot choose my brothers and sisters. I acknowledge that I am a Christian and still a person with strengths and weaknesses. I realize that I find comfort in the hope that someday I will be perfect in the eyes of God. My role as a Christian is not easy but I embrace it with all my heart.

I AM A CHRISTIAN (29)

I am a Christian
And not a very good one.
I say this humbly.

I don't always act like a Christian
Don't always say the things I should say.
Don't always do the things I should do.

I am a Christian
I fall short of the glory of God
By his grace I am called a Christian.

I am a Christian
Who wants to be true and real.
But I'll never be as true as my Lord.

I am a Christian
Who can't wait to go to heaven.
A place where my Lord will make me whole.

I AM A FATHER (30)

Moral: With this poem I acknowledge the joy of being a father and the challenges of the responsibilities. Although I speak of my father being absent I do not judge him because I understand now how difficult life can be. Life brings us challenges that are extremely difficult to endure. Consequently, we make mistakes and we should have the courage to say I am sorry. Being a father is much harder than people think. If men knew what they were up against, I don' think they would try.

I AM A FATHER (30)

I am a father who tries to do his best.
I am not perfect so I try to improve.
I've made mistakes; I've said I'm sorry.

I am a father who wants to do more than provide.
I want to leave a legacy of hard work and ethics.
I am a father, a lucky one, with very good children.

When I was a child I was not with my father.
I am a father who will never leave his children.
I don't hate my father for having left me.

I am a father at school.
I call my students "mijos" and "mijas".
Some address me as Dad.

I am a father and I have a heavenly Father.
Who loves me in ways I cannot explain.
When I'm in trouble I know HE is there.

I AM A HUSBAND (31)

Reflection: Being a husband is another challenge. It is difficult to learn how to love your spouse, especially to love her the way she needs to be loved. Recently I watched a film called "Fire Proof", a story about a firefighter that is fighting to keep his wife. The main theme of the movie is about a book called the Love Dare that was given to the firefighter by his father. I have tried the Love Dare and I am hoping, praying that it will work for me too.

I AM A HUSBAND (31)

I am a husband who dearly loves his wife.
I am a husband, privileged to have a wife.
I am a husband who tries and tries his best.

I am not perfect as you might suspect.
But I try and try to do my best
As my wife can surely attest.

I am a husband who prays for his wife.
A husband who thanks God for his wife.
Who prays for protection against divorce.

I want to grow older with my wife.
At the end of the road I want to hear
That all her dreams came true.

I want to bless my wife.
Don't want to be a burden to her.
Help me Lord to continue loving my wife.

I AM A MILLIONAIRE (32)

Rational: This poem is more than just positive thinking. I am foretelling my future and taking action to make this happen. I sold my car, started riding the bus and purchased a program called Transforming Debt into Wealth. I stopped using credit, I am buying everything cash and I am spending wisely. Besides no credit, cash only and being wise I am also investing. My book "Riding the Bus" might be the answer to a swifter way to debt freedom.

I AM A MILLIONAIRE (32)

From the moment you say you are,
You are what you say you are.
You just have to start doing
What that person you said you are, does.

I am a millionaire from this moment on.
One dollar, one million, what's the difference?
999,999 dollars, that's all.
The principle for one dollar is the same.

I am a true millionaire.
A credit free millionaire.
I owe nothing to no one.
I see an opportunity to make one dollar,
Honestly and legally, I do it.

I am the real owner of
My house, my car, my income.
I am truly a blessed man.

I AM A TEACHER (33)

Reflection: In life we play several roles. Your profession is another role you play. I chose to be a teacher, a French teacher, at age 13. Some of the people who influenced me the most were teachers and it only made sense to give back. I was grateful to the people who were influential in my life and encouraged me not to give up. Life has never been easy and it never will be for me or for anyone else. We have to do our best at whatever role we play.

I AM A TEACHER (33)

I am a teacher, a life changer.
I can affect students in a positive way.
I need to be careful what I say to them.

Many students see school as
A home away from home.
They come to school to feel good.

I am a teacher, who tries
To make school interesting.
I tell corny jokes and laugh myself.

I teach the same thing over and over again
In hopes that students will learn
I point out mistakes and show them the right way.

I am a Spanish/French teacher.
I write Spanish and French educational songs.
I take students to Spain and France.

I am a teacher

I FORGIVE MY FATHER (34)

Moral: Forgiveness is the key to freedom. I shed tears when I wrote this poem. I could think of so many things that my father did that he shouldn't have done and those he didn't do that he should have done. Unfortunately, we humans can recollect the bad things that happen more than the good. After all was said and done the only thing I could think of is that forgiving my father was the only right thing to do.

I FORGIVE MY FATHER (34)

I forgive my father for not protecting me
I forgive my father for not feeding me
I forgive my father for abandoning me
I forgive my father for beating my mom
I forgive my father for not providing for me

I forgive my father for not encouraging me
I forgive my father for discouraging me
I forgive my father for not supporting me
I forgive my father for not teaching me self-defense
I forgive my father for not buying me toys

I forgive my father for not buying me a violin
I forgive my father for not giving me private lessons
I forgive my father for making me angry
I forgive my father for annoying me with the Bible
I forgive my father for talking so much about God

I forgive my father for not giving me confidence
I forgive my father for embarrassing me
I forgive my father for being absent when I needed him the most.
I forgive my father for making me feel guilty
I forgive my father, it's the right thing to do.

I FOUND MY PASS (35)

Reflection: Parents tend to be quite severe when their children lose things especially when it involves money. We tend to forget that we lose things too. An EZ Transit Pass with MTA costs 84 dollars and it's a lot of money to lose during a time of economic downfall but we should never lose our temper with our children. After my daughter lost her bus pass I lost mine a few weeks later. It wasn't until I lost my pass that I was able to look in the mirror and it was difficult to pass judgment on my daughter after the fact.

I FOUND MY PASS (35)

Material things can be found or replaced.
I found my pass in the inside handle of my car.
But sublime things should never be lost.

I found my pass and my dignity.
It is very easy to judge others,
When they do something wrong.

Until I lost my pass too, I realized
I shouldn't judge my daughter
For losing something I lost too.

It is a human phenomenon to lose things
But things can be sought out and found.
Look for it and you will find it.

I found my pass, but I also found
What I already knew, that I am not perfect.
That I can lose and find things too.

I HATE MY FATHER (36)

Moral: Growing up without my father was difficult especially when I envied other boys who had the company of their fathers. I developed hateful feelings as I saw my best friend enjoying life with his father. His entire family seemed to me like a paradise. To this day I consider my best friend somewhat of a brother and his parents like angels. I thank God that, today, I love my father.

I HATE MY FATHER (36)

"I hate my father",
I told my best friend's father,
"For leaving me, being irresponsible".

"No son, never say that
About your father.
You don't know his whole story".

I envied my best friend and his family.
Hot hand-made tortillas, beans and eggs.
I only wanted to be at his house.

I grew to love them as my own parents.
When I went up north, I always
Went to visit, excusing myself
For looking for my best friend.

Then the inevitable came.
My father died, then my mother.
At the funeral I told my surrogate parents

"If it wasn't for you, I could say
I no longer have parents."
Then my eyes became engulfed with tears.

I love my father.

I HAVE A PROBLEM (37)

Reflection: Our problems seem to keep us turning our tires in the mud. Most of us dwell too much on the problem and we forget that there is a solution. Think back to all the challenges you have faced in life. Aren't they just like memories? When you are going through a problem it isn't easy so dwell on the solution rather than the problem.

I HAVE A PROBLEM (37)

Every problem has a solution.
I'm going to search diligently
Until I figure out what to do.

I am not one to give up easily.
I try and try until I come out ahead.
I have a solution, not a problem.

I have a problem.
Not bigger than me.
A problem much smaller than me.

A problem not bigger
Than my greater power.
If faced with adversity, no problem

I HAVE FAITH IN YOU (38)

Message: When I started writing my poems and riding the bus two years ago I was encouraged by one of my students when I shared with him that I would someday publish my poems. I dedicated a poem to him for being an inspiration. As I am writing these lines I am thinking about him and how he might be doing. I hope he learned to deal with his problems in positive ways. Maybe I will hear from him when my book comes out.

I HAVE FAITH IN YOU (38)

i have faith in you mr
a student once said to me
something that a teacher would say to a student

everyone needs someone to believe in
perhaps he is paying me back
for all the times i have encouraged him

i have faith in you he said
which left a warm feeling in my heart
confirming that faith can get things done

i have faith in you
are words i should repeat
to someone faced with a great feat

when i accomplish my next great dream
i will remember the words of my student
"I have faith in you, Mr."

I HAVE FEET (39)

Message: This is a simple message. We have so much to be thankful, for example, our feet. Now that I ride the bus I have the opportunity to walk a lot. When I had my Tacoma I also had a membership at 24Hour Fitness and if I told you I went once a month to exercise I would be lying. It's funny how something good can result from something bad. I am saving money and getting exercise thanks to the fallen economy, and my feet.

I HAVE FEET (39)

I discovered I have feet.
I can walk, go places.
Walk to the store, go for a walk.

We are so spoiled in this country.
We all want to drive nice cars,
Even though we can't afford'em.

I have feet! I discovered.
I can walk from home to the bus,
From the bus to work.

The health spa? What for?
I get cardio vascular every day,
Walking up and down those streets and hills.

Yes, I have feet and they hurt,
But at least I can feel them.
Thank God, I have feet to walk.

I LOVE MY DAUGHTER (40)

Moral: Relationships are extremely important, especially those relationships we have with our family members. My daughter brought so much joy to my life and I should always remember that. I wish I could give her everything she wanted but of course that would be impossible and unnecessary. I believe it is more important that she learn to live within her means. My daughter is now at Parsons, The New School in Manhattan. This is her dream school and she will be 200,000 dollars in debt when she graduates.

I LOVE MY DAUGHTER (40)

I love my daughter, very easy to say.
I love my daughter, I assure you I do.

She speaks of going to a prestigious college
I tell her to go to a school that she can afford.
“I will not get an equity loan
To pay for your school, mija.”

I love my daughter, very easy to say.
I love my daughter, I assure you I do.

She has Sundance, Soap Channel, and BBC America
Animal channels, history channels.
Private art lessons, art materials,
I buy her only what I can afford.

I love my daughter, very easy to say.
I love my daughter, I assure you I do.

I want to teach my daughter
The value of working and spending money
I love my daughter, very easy to say.
I love my daughter, I assure you I do.

I LOVE MY GOD (41)

Moral: I can fool myself, I can fool others but I can't fool God. I love God so much because he has been with me even when I thought he wasn't there. There have been times in my life that I came to doubt the existence of God but he never stopped believing in me. Everything I am and my level of success I attribute to the love He has for me. How could I not love him back?

I LOVE MY GOD (41)

I love my God, I honestly try.
I love my God, he's so good to me.
I love my God, and I fear Him too.

I love my God, He is worthy of praise.
He loves me, protects me, and provides for me.
I love my God, 'cause He loved me first.

I love my God in the best way I know,
I'm not perfect, but God loves me even so.
I love my God, He forgives all my sins.

I love my God and obey his commands.
He knows what is best, I trust Him, I do.
I love my God, 'cause he knows what is to come.

I love my God, onto eternity I will.
He said He would save me and take me to Him.
I love my God, He knows I do.

I LOVE MY SON (42)

Reflection: Love is a feeling that people are generally afraid to express and when we share it we distrust it. Loving my son is another expression of my love, I want to love, and I need to love. Loving my son hits a soft spot in my heart because I grew up without my father. Although my father told me once or twice that he loved me it was difficult to believe since he didn't live with me. When I got married I swore I would never leave my wife or my children.

I LOVE MY SON (42)

Sounds like a cheap cliché of words.
That's because it's hard to explain.
The joy that my son has brought to my life.

It's like me becoming a child again.
Recovering the childhood I once lost.
Reliving my life, doing it better this time.

I guess this is why
I want the best for my son.
Want to be the father I didn't have.

I love my son, amongst the top of his class.
"A"s and "B"s, top violinist in his school.
Advanced in all his CST tests.

I love my son, good son,
Polite to adults, exemplary behavior
His teachers never complain, always delighted.

I love my son, he has big dreams,
To be a professional, virtuoso violinist.
And I will help him accomplish his dream.

I LOVE MY WIFE (43)

Moral: Loving my wife is another task that I accept wholeheartedly. It is not easy to love her at times and I sort of understand why my father couldn't live with my mother. They were both good people but they seemed not good for each other. Maintaining a positive relationship is not easy; it is work. If you love your wife you will do whatever it takes to keep the fire alive.

I LOVE MY WIFE (43)

Hard economic times these days.
Hard to show love when money is short.
Only kind of love is tough love.

I love my wife, she claims I don't,
The way she needs to be loved.
I give my all, not good enough.

After this crisis is over
Things will be better for her and me.
I pray my love she will feel.

I love my wife, you know,
She cleans, she cooks, washes
And irons my clothes.

She is not always in a good mood.
It is then I need to prove,
That I love my wife with all my heart.

She is not always in a bad mood.
When she is happy and content,
I long for a moment of quality time.

I "REALLY" FORGIVE MY FATHER (44)

Message: Has it ever happened to you that you were not really finished when you thought you were? In numerous occasions I had conversations with my father about my childhood, the need for a father figure. In several occasions I had told him that I had forgiven him. It wasn't until my son was born that the pain resurfaced. Now the time came to ask my father to forgive me, and then I was finished.

I "REALLY" FORGIVE MY FATHER (44)

"I'm going to beat your mother
In front of you, before your own eyes.
I am going to leave you
And I will not provide for you."
Is this what my father was thinking,
When he first took me into his arms?

"This is my son. He will be great, a leader.
He will be my pride. I will love him
He will be the one who will give me posterity."
I'd like to think that these are the words
He was thinking when he took me into his arms.

I realized my father was not God
He was only a man, imperfect like me.
I drove north to tell him I really forgave him.
"Father, I came here to tell you that I forgive you,
But not anymore. I am here to ask you to forgive me".
We cried together, four years later, he passed away.

I'M A LUCKY GUY (45)

Reflection: Life is what you perceive it to be. I consider myself a lucky guy simply because I am at a good high school, closer to my house. I was looking for a school where students would be receptive, willing to learn, helpful parents. I am not saying that I didn't have that at my former school but here my cup was overflowing. It was at this school where I was able to realize my dream to take students to Europe.

I'M A LUCKY GUY (45)

I wasn't looking but I found it.
The best things in life,
You just stumble upon.

No summer jobs at my then current school.
Made 3 lazy calls, Garfield, Roosevelt, and Wilson.
Wanted to be close to home, less driving.
Was offered a position to teach CAHSEE Math.

I gave the first test and several students failed.
Called home to assign after school tutoring.
To my surprise, over 20 students showed.

Wow! I couldn't believe it. "I like this school!"
"By any chance, do you need a French/Spanish
Teacher?", I asked the assistant principal.

"Actually I do", he replied, and offered me a job.
I'm a lucky guy, good students, and good teachers
Close to home, I can even take the bus.

IN THE NAME OF JESUS (46)

Moral: This poem is obviously about Jesus. Although miracles happen all the time and everywhere, I attribute my miracles to Jesus. My family, my college degree, my progress are all miracles. Now I am expecting another miracle and that is the publishing of my book and my quest to be financially debt-free. I am expecting a miracle that my book will truly bless others.

IN THE NAME OF JESUS (46)

In the name of Jesus
In no other name
Can miracles be made.

In the name of Jesus
I set out each day.
To meet the toils of the day

In the name of Jesus
I go to work every day and return
Safely home at the end of the day.

In the name of Jesus
I am a father, husband,
Teacher, brother, leader.

In the name of Jesus
No other name has the power
For sinners to find their way.

In the name of Jesus
In no other name
Can miracles happen.

INTOXICATING SMILE (47)

Moral: Teaching is one of the most important roles I play. While my own children are extremely important, as a teacher I have the potential to affect hundreds of students. Teachers have the opportunity to inspire students and to become positive members in their communities. Sometimes we are not sure we are doing our best and other times we may be helping in ways we do not conceive. Teaching is definitely more challenging than many people believe.

INTOXICATING SMILE (47)

Fun teacher, creative, funny
Telling his corny jokes
Trying to make the class interesting

Telling his stories about life
Trying to motivate unwilling students
To do their best in life and school.

He surveyed the room, faces
Suddenly the intoxicating smile
That made him feel he was doing
The right thing and the wrong thing
At the same time.

I asked her once, "Do you hate your father,
For leaving you and your mother when you were still little?"
"Mr.", as was customary for students to call me
"Why should I waste my time hating others?"

Words of gold and wisdom
She became my teacher.
At that point I knew, I was sure
I was doing the right thing.

"KOREXICAN" (48)

Reflection: Prejudice is a tough subject. It hurts people and leaves a permanent mark in a person. People do not choose their race, they are born that way. Bullying someone for race, culture, personal preferences is a denial that not all people can be the same nor should they be the same. Diversity in our schools and in society is a good thing. We have come a long way since human slavery but the road is not finished, we have to travel some more.

"KOREXICAN" (48)

"Chino, chino-japonés,
come caca y no me des",
The little kids would shout at me.
I grew up in a world of prejudice.

Even in the streets of Tijuana
I was expected to speak Chinese.
Fourth generation, of mixed people,
Descendants of Korean immigrants,

Never learned to speak Korean.
Now that I am older,
My dual race is my pride.

I love it when people ask me,
Where are you from?
Unfortunately, racism is still

Alive and well today.
Sometimes I hear negative conversations
When people don't think I understand.

I look really Asian to most people.
Then I blow them away when I tell them
That I lived in France and I speak French too.

LET IT BE DONE (49)

Message: The things that we want in life have to be made to happen. If we see an opportunity it has to be taken. One of my students became very motivated when I told her, "You cannot lose if you never give up." The things that are worth anything in life require effort. The minute you stop trying you lose.

LET IT BE DONE (49)

When you make up your mind
Make up your mind to make it happen.
Whatever it takes, whatever the cost.

Pharaoh's favorite saying was
"So let it be written, so let it be done"
Say what you are going to do and do it.

Set high goals that are difficult to accomplish.
Do not be ordinary, go beyond.
With faith in your hands, knowing that it will happen.

"So let it be written, so let it be done."
Lay down your decree and believe.
Set out to accomplish goals, conquer dreams.

Remember, it won't be easy.
There will be problems, obstacles,
But the final draw will be when you succeed.

LOST PASS (50)

Moral: It is easy to be hard on someone who loses something until it happens to you. In particular we tend to be hard on our children when it comes to money. I was lucky to not have said anything hurtful to my daughter that I would later regret. It took my losing my own pass to remind me who I was: imperfect like anyone else.

LOST PASS (50)

"Mija, can I have my pass?"
"I left it in the car", she said.
I looked everywhere in the car,
Cleaned it out but could not find it.

For the coming weeks I paid
Twenty dollars more out of my pocket.
I was very quick to judge, thought I wouldn't
Lend the pass to her anymore.

I should not have judged her so quickly,
'Cause then unexpectedly I lost my pass.
I had left it in my other change of clothes.
I spent a few more dollars the rest of the week.

If you lose something, don't lose your dignity.
Material things can be found or replaced.
Make sublime things a part of you.
Hide them deep in your heart and soul.

Where they will never get lost.

LOST WALLET (51)

Message: Losing your wallet, purse or something of value can be devastating especially if you are traveling. In times of trouble you can only pray and hope that someone honest will do the right thing. I have been very fortunate lately. I have lost valuable things and I have recovered them. I lost my bus pass on the bus and found my computer on a bench, 40 minutes later, right where I left it.

LOST WALLET (51)

There are all kinds of people
The kind that will steal
The kind that will kill
And the kind that are honest.

If you found a wallet
Stashed with a bunch of money
Would you turn it in to the proper authorities
Or would you keep it for yourself?

It's good to assess your values
Every once in a while
Because you never know
Maybe you will lose your wallet.

The woman got up from her seat
Took the wallet wedged between the seat and the wall
And handed it to the bus driver.
I remembered when I lost my wallet in Biarritz.

LOVE AND FEAR (52)

Moral: Love takes all fear away. If you love to play the guitar and sing, the fear goes away when you perform for others. If you truly love someone, you won't be afraid to say I love you. Fear holds us back and love is the power that moves us forward.

LOVE AND FEAR (52)

If I have fear, my love is not complete.
If I have doubt, my faith is not complete.
If I'm afraid for today, I lack love.

If the phone rings
And my heart thumps with doubt
My love is not complete.

Love and fear cannot abide.
One cancels the other
If I'm afraid to take control,
My love is not complete

If I love, I cannot fear.
If I fear, I cannot love.
Do not fear what tomorrow will bring,

Because God loves you.
God's love is complete
Because God does not fear.
Surrender your fear to God

And He will give you courage to love.

LOVE IN THE PAST (53)

Moral: Love is a strong emotion and often times confusing. Love can be an emotion that will overwhelm you. I have come to a point in my life where I learned to love what is practical. Your emotions will often deceive you, therefore, thinking with your brain may be better than thinking with your heart, although you need both.

LOVE IN THE PAST (53)

When I was six I was in love.
I made her a play table and chairs.
And had the bleeding fingers
To show for it.

Then I fell in love in junior high
She wasn't really that pretty
But there was something special about her
I never told her.

The high school years were traumatic
Fell in love several times
Could poke them on the side with my finger
Joke around, throw papers
But I could never say I love you.

In college, there was no more love.
It was just partying.
Trying to stay on top of my grades
Trying to pursue my career.

As an older man I fell in love
Not with my heart, but with my brain.
Now I've loved my wife,
For 18 years, and for as long as I can.

LOVERS ON THE BUS (54)

Moral: Anyone who rides the bus would agree that there is a wide array of people on the bus. People can display anger, hate, love and sometimes too much love. In today's day and age there seems to be a loss of a sense of decency. People seem to be losing the concept of privacy and respect. I believe that a public bus is not the right place to give passionate kisses.

LOVERS ON THE BUS (54)

This is kind of gross.
Maybe I shouldn't include
This poem in my book.
You see all kinds of stuff

At the bus stop and on the bus.
How much display of love
Should people show on the bus?
Should they be giving passionate kisses?

Tongues fighting each other at each stop?
I think it's a little too much.
Hugging, holding hands is ok,
But out right display? Questionable.

There are more private places for that.
Do I sound like an old man?
Maybe 'cause I am.
What happened to the good old days?

When boys and girls anticipated their first kiss?

LUCKY PEN (55)

Reflection: Right about the time I was going through major changes in my life I came across a pen that impressed upon me a decision that was inevitable. I got the feeling that this pen represented the beginning of a new me, a person who made his mind up to get things done. I know that when you want something you have to work for it but at the same time I think that things just fall in the right places. We just have to make them work. How did I know that my trips would finally succeed during an economic down-turn, that I would sell my car, ride the bus, use my lucky pen to write poems that would later become a book?

LUCKY PEN (55)

Material things don't have intrinsic value
but I once found a pen that has motivated me a lot
it was given to me by a student
who said that the pen was too fancy.

I used the pen to jot down the details,
the details to a long-awaited trip to Europe
it was from that moment that I said
"this pen is going to Paris."

More than a year later
the pen has gone to Paris twice
it has been with me
through the good and the bad times.

Now I am planning the third trip.
this pen is going back to Paris
one time I lost the pen
and a faithful student brought it back.

One day before my departure to Paris.

MAN CROSSING (56)

Moral: Riding the bus has given me time to look at people, observe them, and think about them as I would at a "terrace d'un café" in Paris. With my eyes slightly closed as if wanting to take a nap I observed a man cross the street at a bus stop. I began to think about his life, where he was going, or whether he was married and a father. I might have said a little prayer for him. Every individual has a story to tell, perhaps a book waiting to be written.

MAN CROSSING (56)

Early in the morning
I saw a man crossing the street.
Sitting in my cozy bus seat,
I began to think about the man.

Where is he going, to work?
Is he married, have children?
Is he rich, or buried in debt?
Is he poor and forced to walk?

Life has many twists and turns.
Where will life take the man?
Does he have solid future plans?
Often, I wonder where people are going.

It is important to know where you are going.
Important to know what you are doing.
I'm riding the bus right now,
Taking my son to Hollywood to play violin.

MAN DOWN, GOD UP! (57)

Reflection: I am speaking from a Christian perspective. Too many people want to take control of their lives and others. I believe it is not so much about taking control as much as it is giving control to the right person. I give control to God. I don't want to be guided by my inner man, a man who wants to take control. In extreme circumstances men who want to take control may lose control and hurt others. In this resent economic crunch one too many men have assassinated their wives and children in cold blood and some committed suicide thereafter.

MAN DOWN, GOD UP! (57)

If you want success, be humble.
If you want progress, look up!
Too many people try to take
Their lives into their own hands.

I choose to come down to earth
And look beyond where God is.
I must decrease and He must increase.
I must be small and He must be big.

Pride comes before a great fall.
Wisdom has spoken and you should listen.
Humility comes before success.
No reason for pride, except a BIG GOD.

Now come down to reality, God's reality.
Where 100% depends on Him.
Put your inner man down and God up!
After all, everything you are or have belongs to Him.

MAN PLAYING WITH BOTTLE (58)

Moral: Have you ever felt that you were weird, different from everyone else? In essence we are all different and may seem weird to others. Yet there are those who think we are God's gift to the earth and they admire us. I can prove to you that I am different. I am probably the only one editing my poems at 7:06 am on a public bus.

MAN PLAYING WITH BOTTLE (58)

I often think I am different, weird.
For example, I usually tap my foot
Or move my head to the sound
Of someone else's music.

I am a musician, so I make music
By tapping on things, flicking a paper
I notice that most people just sit there
Doing nothing, blank stare, barely moving.

Then I noticed a man with a plastic bottle
Making excruciating noises by squeezing it
I saw myself, not being able to keep still
I have to doing something, like writing this book.

Then I remembered when I used to drive
I would take my plastic bottle and imagine
That I was playing the snare drum
I felt like going to the man,

"Excuse me sir, can I borrow your snare drum?

MAN RUNNING IS PLACE (59)

Reflection: At first when I wrote this poem I thought this man was quite eccentric, weird. I imagined that it should be quite embarrassing for him to be exercising at the bus stop in front of so many people. Then I began to feel embarrassed when I thought of all the money I threw away at the health spa just to tell my acquaintances that I was a member and I had to make an effort to get to the gym.

MAN RUNNING IS PLACE (59)

I walked up to the bus station
To find a man running in place.
I looked around, right, left, behind
Looked back again to see
Man, still running in place.

I got up to walk around,
To survey the place.
Looked back and the man,
Still running in place.

I wonder what people thought.
Is he crazy? Mentally deranged?
10 minutes transpired,
The man still running in place.

Time passed, maybe 10 minutes more,
The man still running in place.
The bus finally arrived,
And the man stopped,

Running in place.

MAN-UP! (60)

Moral: I consider this poem to be the opposite of my poem about giving God control. Too many of us try to take control for the wrong reasons such as insisting in our own way. Men who try to act like men may not realize that some things are out of our control. I believe a real man will give God control especially when the going gets tough. I want to trust God with my problems.

MAN-UP! (60)

"Man up!" the text said.
At first, I didn't get it.
Get tough, do what men do.

I have a problem with that.
Men who try to act like men
Often commit atrocities.

I'm already a man,
God made me a man.
God wants me to be His man.

Just because the economy is bad
I'm not going to kill my wife and children.
Men sometimes commit
Horrendous crimes when they take control.

Next time things get tough,
I'm going to get rough, with God.
A man looking up to God
"Man-up!", he texted.

Man down, and God up!
I'm trusting God for my problems.

MINI "CHOLOS" (61)

Moral: Bullying hits a soft spot in my heart because it involves my son; and it brings back memories from my childhood and the bullying I endured. Of course, bullying is a social evil, no matter who it is happening to. It doesn't matter if the bullying is due to race, color, sexual orientation; there is no excuse for it. My son stood his ground and he had to defend only once. Today he is blessed with LACHSA a school where it is ok to be different.

MINI "CHOLOS" (61)

"You blanken blanker!", they shouted.
Three boys from Tracy Elementary
Maybe 5th or 6th graders,
As tall or slightly taller than my son.

"Hey stupid white boy"!
Three boys totally strangers,
Wanting to fight with my son
For no reason at all.

My son knows how to defend,
Block, kick, and jab in the right place.
One or two contacts per kid
And they'll be down on the floor.

This time he's not alone
One tall girl, and two tall eighth grade boys
"Shut up you stupid little mother effers!"
Don't make us go there and kick the "blank" out of you."

The two tall boys approached
The three little kids
And chased the mini "cholos" away.

MY CHOICE (62)

Moral: Life is full of choices. People can choose to do right or do wrong. This economic crunch has caught everyone by surprise, including me. Few Americans have money set aside for emergencies. Thanks to hard economic times I learned my lesson. Today I am preparing for the next rainy day. The money I save through public transportation and my frugal spending has put me on the right road to economic freedom. I feel for those people who don't have a choice; they have to ride the bus.

MY CHOICE (62)

It is my choice.
I choose to ride the bus.
I choose to save money,
By riding the bus.

I choose to save
Money for retirement.
I choose to become
Debt free and financially free

Save 400 dollars per month in gasoline.
Save 4800 per year.
48,000 in ten years.
Invest, multiply, "triplify".

I do not want to be
Forced to live like a poor man,
When I am old and sick.
I do not want to be a burden.

You have a choice too.
What do you want in life?
Fame, honor, success?
Well, choose to get it.

MY DAUGHTER'S TEARS (63)

Reflection: My daughter came home one day burst into tears and ran to her bedroom. I went up to her room and my wife followed inquiring what I had said to her. I had only asked how her day went and soon found out she had been betrayed. My daughter is an over achiever and she was stressed with school and a boy who was pressuring her. Although it hurt, my daughter was strong and she sent him on his merry way.

MY DAUGHTER'S TEARS (63)

"He told me he accidently
kissed another girl", she cried.
Her heart was broken.

"I have two AP tests.
Don't think I am prepared", she sobbed.
"Let's pray, mija", I said.

"Dad I'm working so hard,
What will I do? Parsons is my dream".
"All you can do is try", I assured.

I won the war with my daughter.
She is determined to be successful, a fashion designer.
She takes AP classes and maintains a 3.5 GPA

"I didn't finish my homework, Dad",
Tears running down her cheeks.
"Can't concentrate, can't get enough sleep."

"You know mija? When I was in school
I endured several sleepless nights,
It just hurts more to see you cry"

NINE TIMES (64)

Message: I believe people give up too easily. If you really want something you can't give up. I really want to sell this book, make money and help people on the way. If you are reading this book, you know I made it. I am working on book number 2 now. I am not going to give up until my dream to become a writer comes true too. You shouldn't give up on your dream either.

NINE TIMES (64)

How many times should someone try again?
After how many times does someone give up?
Does a successful person try and try until he succeeds?

Had a learning disability and didn't know it.
Struggled through school, A's and B's, sleepless nights.
Graduated but he couldn't pass the entrance exam.

Took extra classes, seminars, paid money.
Took test once, twice, thrice, didn't pass it.
Took more seminars, still couldn't pass it.

Takes the test for the eighth time.
Got 122 points, passing score was 123.
Very discouraged, settles for a different career.

Five years later the dream resurfaces.
Takes the test again, without studying.
Passes the test with 123 points.

Goes back to college to finish career.
Discovers disability and gets help.
I wonder if he would have taken the test 10 times.

NON-OPERATION (65)

Rational: If something is not in use we should not have it or be paying for it. Before I could put my car on non-operation status I sold it, took the money and paid off my wife's Chrysler. I considered that I would be saving not only on gasoline and insurance but monthly payments and interest, not to mention no accidents or car repair. I am fighting back; this crunch will not asphyxiate me.

NON-OPERATION (65)

I can't afford new tires.
I can't afford a new bicycle.
I want to save money on gasoline.

I continued thinking.
Why should I pay insurance
On a car I am not using?

30 dollars per month for storage.
Why should I store
Something I am not using?

I am going to put my car
On non-operation status.
I should not be paying insurance

On something I am not using.
I am a millionaire
And I should think like one.

ODE TO MY ANGELIC FATHER (66)

Moral: Since I did not have my own father when I was growing up I believe God blessed me with several fathers. I don't know why but ever since I was a child I always wanted to be with people older than me and I looked for mentors: father figures who would help me. Even as an older man I look up to people who are older, whether it is a year or ten years. I can benefit from the experience they have to share. An old drunkard on the bus is giving me advice, "Don't drink!"

ODE TO MY ANGELIC FATHER (66)

I am a very blessed man.
I came to Los Angeles
A total stranger, and I was admitted
To his home and became like a son to him.

Trusted me to share his home
With two older brothers
And two teenage sisters
Became a member of the family.

He became like a father to me
He gave me advice
Listened to my problems
I adopted him as my own father.

I am a blessed man.
His 50th wedding anniversary came
String quartette, Bach, Beethoven, Tchaikovsky
Mozart, I was a guest of honor.

Every Father's Day, he is sure
To get a call from me.

ODE TO MY FRENCH-BASQUE FATHER (67)

Message: The next series of poems are my favorites. They deal with the men who have molded me into the man I have chosen to become. They all contributed to my life in very special ways. My French-Basque father was instrumental in the survival of the teenage years. I loved him more that I could express. I believe that I can thank him that I am a French teacher today.

ODE TO MY FRENCH-BASQUE FATHER (67)

I have been such a lucky, blessed man!
During the crucial years of my father's absence
God sent me a French-Basque father.

An old man of about 70
No son of his own.
Took me under his wing, taught me French.

I'm a lucky man
To have had a French-Basque father,
Who taught me values and French culture.

Boiled, sautéed mushrooms
Side of mutton, artichokes, grapes
French bread and a glass of red wine.

Then I went to Biarritz, France.
Stayed in his home, he paid part of my way.
It was a sad day when he passed away.

ODE TO MY FRIEND (68)

Reflection: My friend from the fifth grade who I consider my friend to this day is son to one of the mentors I had in my early childhood. I learned to love him (although I didn't call it that then) like a brother and I thought his parents were angels. Even my best friend was an angel sent to me by God to give me the protection I so much needed from the eager bullies who thrilled in making my life miserable. My friend's father made it clear to me that I should not hate or judge my father.

ODE TO MY FRIEND (68)

"From now on, anyone who picks on Louie,
Has to go through me", defended the big fifth grade boy.
He stood with his big frame, arms hanging to the sides.
I'll never forget; the bully called out my friend to a fight.

We went to the back of the school
And my friend flipped the bully on his back.
He hot up, shook hands, and that was the end.
The bullies soon thereafter stopped bothering me.

I learned to play guitar and I taught my friend.
In high school we somewhat drifted away.
I pursued French and books,
He pursued cars, parties, girls.

But a true friend is a friend forever.
When I drove north to my home town
I always tried to look him up.
Then the big 5'0' came around the corner.

I received the well-anticipated call.
"Luis, now that we are older, I wanted to make
A special call and you were
The first person that came to my mind."

ODE TO MY HEAVENLY FATHER (69)

Message: This is one father who will never leave you. This father knows the past, present and future. He knows the hard times you have endured and he knows of the good times to come. Sometimes it may feel that we are alone but that's only because He wants us to learn from our experiences. Next time you go through hard times remember that He loves you and all will be alright.

ODE TO MY HEAVENLY FATHER (69)

When I was a child
My paternal father was absent
But my Heavenly Father was not.

Now that I look back,
I know He was there.
How else did I make it this far?

When times were good
I would walk along side him.
When times were hard
He would carry me in his arms.

I know my heavenly father has
Always been with me
Even when I couldn't feel Him

It was during my hard times
When he was with me the most.
Today He still loves me, protects me and saves me.

ODE TO MY PATERNAL FATHER (70)

Moral: Unfortunately those people whom you would expect to love you the most are those who will oftentimes neglect you the most. A little boy expects a lot from his father. In the crucial early years of his life he wants to know that there is a hero who will protect him. Once we get older we realize that our fathers are not all-powerful gods. We learn to accept them as they are, with their flaws remembering that we ourselves are not perfect.

ODE TO MY PATERNAL FATHER (70)

Although my father was absent
From ages 10 to18,
He was still my father.

Although he did not send money
To feed my brothers, sisters and me
He was still my father.

Although my father beat my mother
And I swore I would kill him someday,
He was still my father.

Although he was not perfect,
A man with many flaws,
He was still my father.

I know down deep inside
My father loved me, he told me so.
He was my father.

When I was older
I connected with my father
How proud he would be
If he could see me today.

OK, YOU WIN (71)

Reflection: I love speaking other languages. I wish I could speak other languages besides French, Spanish and English. Since I am part Korean, someday I would like to learn to speak the language and learn more about that part of my culture. When I reach retirement age if I live long enough I will surely make it my quest to learn to communicate in Korean. Most of my life I have had to convince people that I am from Mexico. I might as well live up to this expectation.

OK, YOU WIN (71)

I walked up to the cash register
Noticed a man was training a woman.
“Are you training a new employee?” I asked.
“Yes, why do you want to know?” he inquired.

“Well, have you taught her the most important thing?”
“Well what do you think that is?” he implored.
“Muchas gracias,” I answered with a smile on my face.
“And you speak Greek too, don’t you?”

“Efcharistó polý” I replied, smiling.
I didn’t know the woman he was training spoke Russian.
She turns and says, “And now you’re going to speak Russian. “
“Bol′shoe spasibo,” I replied, in a continued smile.

Finally they gave out a smile.
“Ok, ok, you win. Muchas Gracias.”
I love speaking other languages,
And love the richness of culture that they offer.

ONE FOOT IN FRONT OF THE OTHER (72)

Message: I love this poem. When you know you are doing your best there is only one way to go and that is forward. There are moments in life when you don't know if things will work out but you have to keep moving forward. Has your life ever been so difficult and confusing that you didn't know what to do? Most people have at one point or another.

ONE FOOT IN FRONT OF THE OTHER (72)

When I am unsure of
Where I am going,
One foot in front of the other.

When I am doing my best,
Things don't seem to work out,
One foot in front of the other.

When I meet an obstacle
That seems to slow me down,
One foot in front of the other.

When depression and disillusionment
Make it difficult to see ahead,
One foot in front of the other.

When others don't support me,
I know God loves me and I put
One foot in front of the other.

When you want to succeed,
In spite of it all, move forward and put
One foot in front of the other.

PERPETUAL GIVER (73)

Moral: This is a very special story of an inanimate object taking on some kind of spiritual form. Some people love their cars so much that they even give them a name. I had promised my son that my Tacoma would be his. I could see myself with my son driving to Cal. St. LA and then driving to Wilson High School to teach French and Spanish. My pickup was my spiritual sanctuary. I would often get sleepy, park somewhere and pray.

PERPETUAL GIVER (73)

I want to sell my Tacoma
To help me pay off my Chrysler.
I'll be saving on insurance, $100
Saving on car payments, $300
I'll be saving on gasoline, $400
Saving 50 dollars on interest.

Why is my Tacoma a perpetual giver?
First of all, I prayed and God gave it to me.
I save 50 dollars per month in interest.
I save 10,100 per year and 101,000 in ten years.
If I never buy a car on credit again,
I will save 50 dollars a month until I die.

How is it perpetual you ask?
If my son and my daughter learn the principle,
If they teach their children how to economize,
As long as there are people on earth,
My family and my posterity will forever
Save 50 dollars a month in interest.

PERSISTENCE 74

Moral: I call this the stupidest poem I have ever written, yet the message is so profound. You know that the winners in this world never give up. One of my students was impressed with the statement, "You cannot lose if you keep fighting". How many people do you know that just gave up on their dream? I am not giving up. I am selling this book and I am going to help those who read it. And don't you give up either!

PERSISTENCE 74

Perhaps the most important key to success.
You cannot lose if you keep fighting.
Even if you die fighting, you are a winner.

It didn't work out the first time, this way?
Do it the second time, this other way.
It didn't work the second time? Go for 3.

It didn't work the third time?
Do it again, and again, and again,
And again, and again, and again, and...

Every time you fail you are really succeeding.
Every time you do it again,
You learn something new from your mistakes.

Every time you will do it better and better,
And better, and better, and better, and better,
And better, and better, and better, and...

Is this clear? I think it is.
Now go do it again, and again, and again,
Until you succeed.

POOR WOMAN (75)

Message: One of the reasons I want to be a millionaire is to bless people like this woman. I want to be a secret philanthropist on a bus, in line at the store and just bless people. Riding the bus has given me so many reasons to be thankful. I wonder about those people who are forced to ride the bus and they have difficulty being thankful even for the bus. I am a lucky guy, I ride the bus because I am smart and I want to and I thank God for all that he has given me.

POOR WOMAN (75)

Poor woman with three small children.
Where is the father, at work?
Where is the father, absent?
Is this family forced to ride the bus?

They seem to be a tight family.
The little sister kisses her little brother.
The third child very talkative.
Baby boy on his mother's lap, a girl on each side.

I wonder if she is finished with children.
I could handle only two, so expensive!
Where three eat four can share.
Only, everyone will eat less.

Poor woman with three small children.
Is she coming from work?
Dropping off children to go to work?
We are blessed, my wife and kids.

POTENTIAL AFTER 50 (76)

Message: Wow! This is probably one of the epic poems in my book. The economy was just beginning to decline. There was talk that there would be fewer opportunities to teach summer school. I was searching for I don't know what, but God knew. It was then when I stumbled on Wilson High School and then things began to happen and the best thing that ever happened to me was the decline in the economy. The fall woke me up, if not I would have slept into retirement and an economic disaster.

POTENTIAL AFTER 50 (76)

I had just turned 50.
I was at my high school's graduation.
Judge Mathis was the keynote speaker.
"Don't wait till you're 50.
For someone to tell you, you have potential."

The words kept ringing in my ears.
It made sense, success was at hand.
Young seniors going out and into the world.
A world of paths to take and decisions to make.

But the words kept coming back to me.
Finally, it hit me hard like a rock on the head.
What's wrong with someone telling me
I have potential at age 50?

There were things I wanted to do.
But I had always been afraid to do them.
I wanted to write rap songs to teach my students.
The words came back to me, "You have potential".
Today I have written two raps, working on my third.

PRAYING (77)

Reflection: The theme of prayer comes up often in my poems. I believe most people are running around like a chicken with their heads chopped off and are not accomplishing much. People just need to stop, relax, think and pray. Riding the bus has given me that edge to take time to pray, to thank God for the little things that may seem insignificant at first glance. I thank God for the driver and my bus.

PRAYING (77)

The bus is a good place to pray,
a place to give thanks,
that someone else is doing the driving.

The woman with three small children,
the man on the wheelchair,
the woman who keeps spitting into a bag.

Lord, I pray for those who are poor,
for those who are ill and destitute,
for those unemployed, in need of money.

Some are poor and are forced to ride the bus,
some cannot drive because they never learned,
but Lord, please watch over them all.

Time to think about tomorrow,
time to reflect upon the past,
time to think about lessons learned.

Lord, I pray for a safe ride home,
pray my family is safe and well,
thank you, for letting me ride this bus.

PROCRASTINATION (78)

Moral: This poem is the opposite of my poem 'Persistence". This poem is dedicated to those people who know what to do but they just need to get up and go. It took me some time to decide to do what I knew was the right thing to do. Maybe I was afraid, concerned about what others would say. Now I am doing many of the things I said I would do and I have so much more to do.

PROCRASTINATION (78)

The economy is bad
I thought I would ride the bus.
I wanted to buy a bicycle,
Could not afford it.

I waited more than a month.
Now I am finally riding the bus.
Thought I would write a book.
Needed to buy a composition book.

Waited and waited, weeks and weeks.
Now I have a composition book
Now I am writing my book.
Nothing is holding me back.

No more procrastination
I am doing what I said I would do
I am riding the bus.
I am writing my book.

I am writing 101 poems and thoughts.
I will not procrastinate.

PURRING OF A CAT (79)

Rational: One of the things I truly enjoy while riding the bus is that I can go to sleep. I suffer from sleep when I drive: the bright sun and slow-moving traffic just knock me out. I remember when my daughter was an infant. I would sometimes take her on a ride to help her fall asleep so I could get back to grading my papers. Now that I ride the bus and I get sleepy I imagine my former cat Topacio close to my ear and I take a well-deserved nap.

PURRING OF A CAT (79)

When I am tired and sleepy
The sound of a cat can
Make me fall asleep.

The soothing sound
That seems to beat
To the rhythm of my heart.

Close my eyes
Allow my head to fall
Where it may.

Thinking, day dreaming
Relaxing, resting, not a worry
Never thought it could be this good.

My cat is long and hard like metal
It has wheels for legs
And its engine purrs like a cat.

READ (80)

Moral: Reading is a problem for me. I like to read only what I like to read or what I want to read. My eyes are going bad now and it is hard to read the small print on medicine and products. Nevertheless, if I don't make the effort it is worse in the end. Please read, read everything that is good for you: self-help books, do-it-your-self books, read the Bible. It will be good for you.

READ (80)

I know how to read, but I don't like
To read the directions on products
Especially the small print.

Consequently, I end up breaking something
Having to hire the plumber anyway.
I need to learn how to read.

When I used to drive I remember reading
One-hour parking, but I didn't read
The other sign, "NO PARKING AFTER 6PM"

I need to learn to read
The small print on zero percent
Credit cards that promise the world.

After the six months
The rate goes to over 20 percent.
If you still owe they charge you all the past interest.

Learn to read the things
You don't like to read
It will save you time and money.

REALITY (81)

Reflection: I have noticed that people who speak of reality are usually those who think negatively. They are the kind of people who discourage dreamers, who question and complain. I believe that a lot of what is real can be fabricated by individuals who have goals and set their minds to accomplish them. Everything that exists, with the exception of God, was invented by somebody. Reality doesn't happen all by itself.

REALITY (81)

You know what reality is?
It is just someone else's idea.
The Wright brothers were laughed at
For trying to fly the first airplane.

Things don't happen in the real world,
Until an idealistic person makes it happen.
Nobody thought Henry Ford could run a car.
Now look at how far the automobile has gone.

Reality is what you think will happen.
Reality is having a dream and making it real.
Realists are pessimists, dooms day people.
Idealists are positive people, even in adversity.

I once dreamed I would graduate high school
College, become a teacher, write music,
Be a performer and entertain people,
Get married, have high-achieving children.

Now I am dreaming that I will be a millionaire.
Do you think this dream will come true too?

SAVING MONEY (82)

Moral: Saving money is one of the most difficult tasks for most people. They say that only 1 percent of the world's population controls the economy. We could narrow the gap if we started living within our means. I sold my car and I am riding the bus because I made an intelligent choice. The use of credit has robbed me of my hard-earned income and it has almost destroyed my marriage. If you don't have the cash, you shouldn't buy it.

SAVING MONEY (82)

Didn't buy the tires,
Didn't buy the bicycle,
I am walking to the bus stop
Walking from the bus to work.

Saved 400 on tires,
Saved 300 on bicycle,
Saving 400 on gasoline,
Saving on future maintenance.

Am I really saving money?
Yes. I am paying 700 per month,
Beginning with my smallest debt,
Until I pay off all, including "the" house.

Compounding interest working against me,
Compounding interest working for me,
I am buying things cash now,
No more 50,000 dollars for a 25,000 dollar car.

SETBACKS (83)

Moral: Life is full of challenges that threaten even the toughest to give up. I can't think of anyone who didn't win by being persistent. Sometimes we can get lucky but we still have to work to keep the ball rolling. The trips I have conducted to Europe have had their challenges but they have been very rewarding. I am now working on my third trip, just weeks away from getting my tax exemption for my 501(c) 3.

SETBACKS (83)

In life there are setbacks
But no reason to give up
Take one step back and two steps forward.

150 dollar late fee
For those who didn't apply on time
It's ok, we're moving forward.

Two students dropped, one moved
It looks gloomy from this end.
Lost three students, we're signing up 6.

Setbacks are part of life
But giving up should not be.
Find a solution, because there is one.

Finally, don't give up.
Keep moving towards the finish line.
And when you get close, engage the kick.

SING AGAIN (84)

Moral: This poem is one of my favorites. It reminds me of the need to try it again especially in the face of discouragement. I often get the feeling that I could be so much better in all the things I do. I will never be perfect but that is no reason to stop trying. Listening to the birds sing on one fresh early morning reminded me how God takes care of the birds: feeds them, clothes them and they never complain.

SING AGAIN (84)

I came to the bus stop this morning,
A little tired and depressed, down on myself.
I can me a better father, husband, teacher, person.
I can be a better provider, have a happier wife.

Then I heard the birds singing and speak.
I heard them sing that everything was fine.
"You're right, you can do better,
Continue trying to do your best. It's ok."

I remembered how God provides for the birds,
And they never complain, they are thankful.
I am going to thank God for what I have:
My job, degree, wife, children, house, the bus.

The birds are singing again
And I'm going to do this again:
A father, a husband, teacher, person, provider.
After all, my God does all the work.

I am his hired helper.

SLOW MOVING MAN (85)

Message: Growing old is part of life but growing poor is not. If we play our dice right even the poorest of us can have a better retired life. You have to prepare for the future, spend wisely, invest, stay away from credit. We need to go back to the old-fashioned days when most people used cash only to buy things they really needed. When I am old I am going to be so well off that I am going to be a "givenaire".

SLOW MOVING MAN (85)

Slow moving man
Sighing at every move
His face wrinkled in knots of pain.

What is a man so sick, so old,
Doing on a public bus?
Can he not afford a car, a taxi?

When I am old, I want to be well off.
I want money coming out of ears
To help every solicitor and peddler

That comes to my door.
It's sad to see a man, so sick, so old.
Holding his stomach with one hand

Holding the railing with his other hand
Ever jerk the bus makes,
You can hear the man moaning and groaning

It's sad to see so many poor people
Riding the bus, not by choice, but necessity.

SMELLS (86)

Rational: This poem is not meant to put down people who ride the bus, but I am sure you can catch the humor. Riding the bus can be a challenge in many ways. While it can be fun to meet and talk to people sometimes we come against a difficult situation not easy to bare. Even so, I thank God that I ride the bus. Riding the bus has helped me appreciate what I am and what I have, especially on challenging days.

SMELLS (86)

Body odor, perfume, gas, alcohol, smoke.
Wait a minute, is that excrement?
Did somebody cut one?

Did he not shower?
Did she just leave
A manual labor job?

Perhaps the man is homeless.
Perhaps the boy was playing sports.
He is all sweaty.

Another price to pay,
For riding the bus,
Besides the bus fare.

Hold your breath, breathe slowly,
Sit next to the window,
Next to the air conditioner, if there is one.

SUFFER OR SUFFER (87)

Moral: As a teacher I have observed the destructive behavior of my students and I have seen those students who are headed for success. Those students who were never taught the value of hard work are left in a world of wrong decisions. Students who listened to positive advice are headed toward their dreams. As a teacher I try to be that missing link and the one who encourages those who are committed to their future.

SUFFER OR SUFFER (87)

In life you have two choices.
You can suffer or you can suffer.
You choose how you want to suffer.

The first is when you
Stay up all night, take drugs, have sex,
Go to parties, fist fight, you're popular!

The second, you suffer for being dedicated,
Stay up all night studying, finishing homework.
Work hard, go to study parties, you are tired.

The difference happens 5 to 10 years later.
You graduated high school, college, got married.
Have a beautiful/handsome spouse, responsible children.

If you have fun first, your future is bleak
10 years later, no spouse, neglected children
No steady job, no money, no dignity.

So, you choose,
Do you want to suffer?
Or do you want to suffer?

SWAYING SIDE TO SIDE (88)

Reflection: This poem alludes to the routine of daily life. There all types of people on the bus seemingly all doing the same thing. You can observe the monotonous motions of people who are staring, thinking, sleeping. You can hear people tell their stories about how they ended up on the bus. My story is about fighting back during a falling economy.

SWAYING SIDE TO SIDE (88)

Heads moving from side to side
Like teeter-totters on a stick
Old, new, young, women, men, boys and girls

Heads turning right and left
The bus prepares to stop
And all heads, bopping forward

The bus finally stops
And all heads jerk back
And we do this again and again

Sometimes a head will sway
Completely to the right or to the left
And suddenly jerk back when startled

Yes, I'm riding the bus too
My head moving in all directions
Suddenly I fall asleep till my head jerks back again

THANK YOU SO MUCH. (89)

Moral: This poem reminds us about the right attitude towards gratitude. You would think that a man on a wheelchair would have very little to be thankful for, but maybe he has learned to appreciate life. He is probably not thinking about his disability, but instead he is thankful that he can move in a wheelchair. For everything we complain about we can find several more to be thankful. The wheelchair man confirmed in my heart that I need to me thankful for what I have.

THANK YOU SO MUCH. (89)

"Thank you so much", said the man on a wheelchair.
Several times he said thank you to the bus driver.
The bus driver brings down the ramp,

And the man on the wheelchair says thank you.
People waiting outside while he boards,
Says thank you to all of us, waiting outside.

Driver secures his wheelchair,
Again, the wheelchair man says thank you.
Wheelchair man reaches his stop,

Thank you so much, thank you, thank you.
Driver detaches his chair
And once again he said thank you.

The driver brings down the ramp
And the wheelchair man says
Thank you so much, thank you, thank you.

I began thinking of the importance of gratitude.

THE ECONOMY IS BAD (90)

Message: As I said before, the economy is one of the main themes of my book. Saving money for emergencies is something most of us fail to do. As part of my debt freedom program saving money for emergencies is instrumental. Putting money in the bank to purchase your next car is like paying yourself and saving on interest. You become your own banker and you handle your own money instead of letting others handle your financial future.

THE ECONOMY IS BAD (90)

The economy is bad for most people.
99 percent live paycheck to paycheck.
No money in the bank.

The economy is bad for those who have debt.
For those who have a lot of things,
That they cannot afford.

The economy is bad for those who get sick
For those who cannot work due to illness,
For those who need employment every month.

The economy is bad for those who lost their job
For those who depend on their income to live.
Those who have extreme debt.

The economy is bad for those who don't save money,
Six times their monthly income to survive,
Who are not prepared for emergencies.

My economy is great!
I have money in the bank.
I don't owe anything to anybody.

THE MEXICAN MOSES (91)

Message: It is unfortunate that in today's day and age people still look at the race of other people and perhaps by instinct we make judgments about how we see others. Many have gone across cultures but often times the cultural shock is not easy. It is difficult to make adjustments for both sides. Consequently, what seemed to be a good idea at first turns out to be quite challenging. We have come a long way since slavery and the concept of human rights but we still have a long way to go.

THE MEXICAN MOSES (91)

"You should go back to your people
And help them succeed",
An Anglo teacher once told me.

Since when did I become
The spokesperson for all Mexicans?
When was I chosen to set Mexicans free?

I left my predominantly white school
And went back to teach in the inner-city,
As they call it, in affluent neighborhoods.

Perhaps a Hispanic teacher is better off
Teaching students who share similar struggles,
Students who are slaves to a lack of education.

I don't think I can qualify to be a liberator
The Mexican Moses for the education of teens.
But I'd like to make a difference.

I dream of raising a group of inner-city winners
Who will take A.P. French, become fluent and pass the test,
Then go celebrate and have dinner with the French President.

THE MEXICAN MESSIAH (92)

Reflection: Here is another poem that explores the issue of racial injustice. Many people see Christianity as a White religion and they fail to remember that Jesus, the founder, is Jewish. Jesus became the savior for the gentiles and the Jews; therefore, race doesn't matter before God. Today people of all races and cultures have adopted Christianity, form Asians, the Middle Eastern, Hispanics and others. Clearly, Christianity is not exclusive to any one race.

THE MEXICAN MESSIAH (92)

A black kid and a white kid
Were arguing in the back of the classroom.
"Jesus was Black, the Bible says
He had hair like sheep, that's black hair."

"No", the white kid rebutted.
"When have you seen paintings
Of a Black Jesus? Even the oldest works of art
Depict Jesus as a White man."

"No, your both wrong", a Mexican kid interjected.
"Jesus was Mexican, man!"
His name is J-E-S-U-S, his dad J-O-S-E,
His mom M-A-R-I-A. Man, I rest my case.

How stupid racism can be.
Race doesn't matter before God.
Jesus is the Messiah, Savior of the World.
He can very easily be "The Mexican Messiah".

TO MY WIFE (93)

Message: Love is a difficult subject. Often, we love but not the way our partner needs it. Love becomes a complex thing even more when you throw in financial and social factors. During these hard, economic times many men have resorted to killing their wives and children rather than face the horrendous reality that they lost their jobs, and material possessions. Something beautiful can quickly turn into something horrible. Ironically the very knife that we use to cut our food to feed our children can also be used take the life of a human being.

TO MY WIFE (93)

It is difficult,
To write a poem to my wife.
What do I say? The usual clichés?
I love you, you're my everything?

It is difficult to put into words,
The gratitude that I feel and owe
To a woman who took interest in me.
There's been good times and bad.

But I have to remember the good days
If I want to enjoy my wife, my life.
It's no coincidence
That wife and life rhyme.

My children, house, and college education,
A few of the things I can attribute to my wife
Do you have a spouse? Don't enrage.
Because life and wife,

Can also rhyme with knife.

TOILET WATER (94)

Reflection: Have you ever done something that you regretted later? Life is a series of ups and downs. It is not shameful to make mistakes but it is a sad cry if you don't face up and deal with them. In this poem I recollect that I had to go back to point A with the intent that I would start all over again. If you make a mistake, it's ok; just learn from it.

TOILET WATER (94)

This is another moment I should not forget.
I was used to getting good grades in high school
But college was my down fall.

After two years of probation I decided
I would take a one-year vacation
To reestablish my goals.

Like many young men I made the mistake,
Bought a new car that ate better than me
Monthly payments and insurance killing me.

I had two jobs to make ends meet.
The packing shed and small private cleaning business.
What I thought would be one year turned to 3 years.

One evening when doing cleaning at a local
Chiropractic office, I saw the reflection of my face
As I leaned over to clean the toilet.

The toilet water spoke to me.
"Is this what you want to do in life?"
Shortly after, I sold my car and went back to college.

WAITING (95)

Message: I have heard my pastor say that everyone gets really excited about faith campaigns but no one ever talks about patience campaigns. The truth is that there is a lot of waiting and hard work before something can happen, often times, even when we exercise our faith. People who have patients don't give up. If you want something really badly you have to be willing to work and wait for the miracle to unfold. Good dreams are worth waiting for.

WAITING (95)

Patience is my greatest asset.
Waiting for the moment of triumph.
Waiting hours, days, weeks, month, years.

Great things take time to mature.
An embryo takes nine months
And look at the miracle that happens.

Patience and faith are sisters.
One waits for the other.
They both have the same heavenly father.

Patience is my best friend.
She walks me through the hard times.
She comforts me when things don't look good.

I keep on waiting, pressing forward.
It's just a matter of time.
Before the inevitable finish line.

Wait don't hurry up.
"Good things come to those who wait"
This proverb is clear, you should wait.

WHISTLE AND WALK (96)

Reflection: This is one of my favorite poems because it is a perfect picture of what life can be. How many times has your life seemed so perfect when all of a sudden you had a great fall such as tripping on a crack on the sidewalk? What is important is not that you fell but that you got up. Life has all kinds of challenges such as health problems, financial problems, but they are just like falling on the sidewalk. You get up and start walking again.

WHISTLE AND WALK (96)

What have I been missing!?
The birds singing, smell of flowers
Cardio vascular, up and down those hills
Morning dew caressing my cheeks.

Dogs barking as I walk by
I've made three friends that don't bark anymore
The usual people I meet, "good morning, sir".

Sometimes I change scenery, different street.
I think and whistle about the money I am saving,
How God has protected me from the very first day.

I thank God for public transportation
I can afford a car but I choose to ride.
Walking and whistling, feeling good,

Suddenly, I trip on a crack on the sidewalk
How can you put a price on that!?
I pick up my pace, and start whistling again.

YES, YOU WILL (97)

Moral: It is so easy to give up on others especially on yourself. As a teacher I have to have faith that something is going to give. If I give up on my students, I am going to have a lot of losing battles. I cannot save all my students, but I have to keep trying to win a few. Sometimes all a person needs, is a little push, a little nudge that shows that someone cares.

YES, YOU WILL (97)

"I will never go to tutoring", he challenged.
"Oh yes, yes you will", I assured.
I never lost the faith.

A teacher should never
Give up on his students
He/she should always believe.

Now my student is coming to tutoring
And bringing his friends too.
He is learning and shooting for a "B".

It is difficult to motivate
Someone who does not see
The value of hard work and dedication.

But I keep pressing on
When someone tells you, "No, I won't",
Say "yes, you will", if you know it's a good thing

YOU ARE FORGIVEN (98)

Message: Currently I am reading a program called, "The Power of Forgiveness". There is power in forgiving others and when you receive forgiveness. I think it is the next best thing to the power of love. I guess you can't forgive someone if you don't have love. If you don't forgive others you are not only hurting them but yourself as well. What a beautiful feeling to know that we are forgiven by grace.

YOU ARE FORGIVEN (98)

"You are forgiven", she said to me.
Months had passed since I lost
My cool with her, her son,
Counselor and principal.

Wrote a letter of apology
Because I knew I had acted
Way out of character.
I apologized again,

Giving no excuses
For the second time,
"You are forgiven."

Her son was a truly
An intelligent young man
We had a misunderstanding.

I apologized to her and her son again
"You are forgiven, forget it.
"You have nothing to worry about."

The Grace of God

YOU DON'T GET WHAT YOU... (99)

Reflection: It is impossible to get everything we want in life. I don't mean that we should settle for the next best thing but we should be thankful first for what we have before we start asking for more. We should instead desire sublime things with intrinsic value. Material possessions come and go but such things as love, wisdom, stay forever. I appreciate what I have and I want more only to be more grateful.

YOU DON'T GET WHAT YOU... (99)

You don't get what you want,
You want what you get.
That's the secret to true success.
Many apply but not all are accepted

Many play hoops but few become pros.
Many violinists, only one Paganini
But it's an attitude of gratitude
That will help you appreciate what you have.

Look around. See others who wished
They had what you don't appreciate.
Everybody wants more and that's our human demise.
Thank God for what you have and he will add to you.

Solomon asked God for wisdom, He gave him all.
Desire more wisdom, more knowledge.
Desire peace, tranquility with God.
And God will give you peace, beyond your understanding.

YOU HAVE TWO PROBLEMS (100)

Message: As a teacher I get to see students change from good to bad, bad to good, bad to worse, and good to better. I know their personal problems get in the way, causing them to slack off in their school work and many take up drugs to deal with their problems. I tell people that they have to deal with their problems the best they can without causing a bigger problem. A problem doesn't go away by taking drugs or getting high.

YOU HAVE TWO PROBLEMS (100)

If you have a problem,
And you let that problem control you,
Now you have two problems.

If you have a messed-up family,
And you let them bring you down,
Now you have two problems.

If you suffer from depression
And you end up taking drugs,
Now you have two problems.

If you come from a poor family,
And you don't get a good education,
Now you have two problems.

"Your problem is not your problem", I once heard.
"Your problem is how you see your problem"
Every problem has a solution.

If you have a problem
And you seek to find
The best possible solution,

You have no problem.

YOU SHOULDN'T BE A TEACHER (101)

Reflection: What a wonderful way to finish my first book of the series, "Riding the Bus". Besides teaching my students I love to motivate them. I love it when they stop to listen to my stories and poems. I can tell they want to take it all in, all at once, but it is practically impossible. Many of the lessons we learned in life are due to having the experience not necessarily the knowledge. This book and these free-verse poems are just about that: inspiration, motivation, dreams coming true.

YOU SHOULDN'T BE A TEACHER (101)

A student once said to me,
"You should not be a teacher, Mr.
You should be a motivational speaker".

My students seem to enjoy my stories.
I try to motivate them with real-life lessons.
Some listen, some don't, but I keep trying.

So, I thought I would put my thoughts
Into poems and publish my first book.
To leave a mark, that I was here.

I believe that teaching is more than subject matter
I believe teachers should motivate students from within.
If a student becomes motivated, there's no stopping.

I have a calling from God to be a teacher.
I know I am not the best I can be, but I try.
I teach by example. If I made it, my students can too.

Endorsements

Riding the Bus" is a great book exposing an author's humble side and inner strengths. I admire Mr. Villalobos' writing capacity and ability to express such deep thoughts. Each poem demonstrates compassion, hope and real facts of life. I strongly recommend this book!
Leticia Valdez. Parent Center Community Representative,
Wilson High School.

"Riding the Bus 1" by Luis Villalobos is the most inspiring book of poetry I have ever read. He captures those little glimpses of life that we all share and gives them meaning."
Bill Cherry, Financial Consultant

"Riding the Bus 1" was an amazing book for me to read. Mr. Villalobos has the great ability to take what one person might perceive as insignificant and create poetry that makes these 'insignificant' moments into such intimate and heartwarming pieces.
Bayani Africa, US Postal Worker

My father's collection of poems has inspired many people he's come across to reimagine the beauty in life and things that many may deem unbeautiful. "Riding the Bus" has insightful things to say about life.
Tanya Celeste Villalobos

Conclusion

I think that this is not the conclusion to my book but a new beginning. Go back and read my poems, mark your favorite ones. I have to tell you that sometimes I feel I wrote this book for myself. When I am sad, angry, tired, discouraged, happy, hopeful; no matter what I like to go back to ground zero and remember my purpose in life.

Certainly, this is not the conclusion of my book or project when you consider that inspiration is a never-ending ordeal. In addition, I have plans to publish Riding The bus 2 – the sequel, Riding The bus 3 – the dream continues, Riding the Bus with Jesus, Andar en Autobús, and Prendre l'autobus. It is my goal to publish one book every year.

Riding the Bus 2 – the sequel will continue the tradition of writing poetry while riding the bus. I will continue to share my experiences, thoughts, memories of good and bad but always from a positive point of view. I will share that there are only two choices in life, and that is to be positive and positive. Riding the Bus 2 – the sequel will be the test of the success of Riding the Bus 1. This project will continue for many years to come therefore, I will have to practice what I teach: never give up no matter what.

Riding the Bus 3 will be a continuation of dreams and the messagdowne of persistence, that I still haven't given up and that I will persist in my quest to become known as the bus rider/writer. At times it can be difficult to continue on one's quest. Sometimes the discouragement outweighs the positive but winners never give up until the end, and the end comes only when we are laid to rest. In my case, the pen will be the last to fall.

"Riding the Bus with Jesus" will be an exclusive book to my Lord Jesus but not exclusive to Christian readers just as all my projected books. As a rule, I like to learn about all cultures. In my repertoire included are books about Islam, Buddhism, and Jewish teachings. I also have the book of Mormon, Seventh Day Adventist and Pentecostal literature. In fact, because I have explored and opened my mind to other ways of thinking eventually I opted to believe in Jesus. Anything else on this subject I will reserve for the publication of "Riding the Bus with Jesus."

Since I do speak Spanish, many of my followers have suggested that I write a book of Spanish poetry. In fact, I already have started my "Andar en Autobus" version of Riding The bus. These poems will not be translations of my English poems because the richness of the Spanish culture offers a source that provides endless imagination. One of my favorite poems is dedicated to a young couple who would park their tamales and champurrado vending station just below the hill supporting the weight of one of the world's best high schools: Woodrow Wilson High School ☺. I am amazed by the diligence of many of our hard-working immigrants.

As you noticed in many of my poems I had the desire to learn a third language and I was fortunate to have had an adopted French-Basque father in my life. In his honor and the admiration I have for French culture I have begun my French counterpart: "Prendre l'Autobus." I have countless memories of my French/Basque father and my travels in France and Europe. Like many cultures, probably all cultures, the French are very misunderstood. It will be my quest to show the world that French culture is in fact rich and beautiful.

So, I will not say good-bye, but see you later. Expect to see all these books I have mentioned, one every year, once a year. As I am sitting here at Starbuck's, I am thinking, "I am going to leave a positive mark in the world of positive thinking, hope and dreams coming true."

About the author

Mr. Luis Pastor Villalobos has been a teacher of French and Spanish for 22 years. He loves to teach and inspire students. He believes that most students are capable of doing so much more than they realize. Life can be very difficult at times and our problems can become obstacles that will keep children, teens, adults and the elderly from accomplishing their goals. Mr. Villalobos is committed to helping people to see the silver lining in every cloud and see the solution for every problem.

Mr. Villalobos is the father of two children, one at Parson's The New School and the other at Los Angeles County High School for the Arts. He is married with his beautiful wife of 19 years and is committed to making family and marriage work out for the good of everyone. Many of his poetry will attest to the importance of relationships and family relations. Success and a quality education should begin in the home.

Finally, this author knows firsthand what it is like to struggle. He came here to the US at the age of ten, to work in the farms of the Central Valley in California. He knows what it is like to survive with little resources under the most gruesome environments. He is living proof that goals can be accomplished when an individual sets his mind to be a winner in life no matter the costs.

Made in the USA
Middletown, DE
07 July 2023

34542007R00076